Best of Luck
Marvin Russell

To Mckenzie.
A wonderful person and
student with unlimited
potential.

Honoring those who served

Alex Chyanosa

A Life Anything But Ordinary

Extraordinary Triumphs Throughout
World War II and Beyond

by Alex R. Chrzanowski

with Marvin O. Russell

Dedication

This book is dedicated to Marvin Russell and the millions of Americans who put their lives on hold in order to serve their country in its hour of need, especially those that gave the ultimate sacrifice.

Acknowledgements

The interviews proved to be the easiest part of writing this book. To say this process has been a learning experience is an understatement. Marvin agreed for me to interview him in early February 2012 and from there the idea of this book was born. To be honest, I am not an author. I am a teacher that enjoys the profession among other hobbies and could not divest all my time and energy to nothing but this book. Looking back, I know how much Marvin wanted nothing else but to see this book to completion. I thank him for being the perfect subject for which to write. This book would not have been possible without the assistance of Debbie McCaulley. I cannot count the hours of research and editing that she put into this final product. Lastly, I know very few eighty-five year olds that navigate a computer better than Mary Carr. Due to the distance between Marvin and me, Mary proved an invaluable part of this process.

She provided Marvin with copies of the manuscript and

then edited based on his feedback. Many thanks to Debbie and Mary for making this dream of Marvin's and mine a reality.

Table of Contents

Prologue

In the fall of 2002, I read that between 800-1200 World War II veterans died every single day. As a high school history teacher, I realized that now was the time if I wanted to link my students with living history before it was too late. I called every assisted living facility in the area in an attempt to find residents whom my students could interview. Over the course of the next few months, my students spent one to two hours interviewing the residents using questions provided by the Library of Congress. They then typed up the responses and submitted them. It proved to be an amazing experience that my students continued to talk about. The students learned first-hand experiences of the Battle of the Bulge, D-Day, Pearl Harbor, the war in Italy, among other war time experiences.

An employee of one of the facilities said to a resident

named Vera, "Tell them what you did during the war." She replied, 'It was my job to entertain the boys!" When I retell this quip again and again, it is met with a chuckle for hopefully obvious reasons. Vera's entertainment of the boys really was more "PG" than it sounded when she made the comment, but that exemplifies the difference in generations and speaks of a perhaps simpler and more "pure" era. Vera attended an all girls college in Atlanta during the early 1940s. The United Service Organization provided events for G.I.s either training at one of Georgia's numerous military installations or passing through to the war zone. Hundreds of thousands of soldiers attended events that provided entertainment and a few hours of respite from the reality they faced. The U.S.O. asked local girls to volunteer at these events where they danced with soldiers or simply made sandwiches. She made it very clear that fraternization was not permitted and any girl caught maintaining a relationship outside of her volunteer duties would not be asked back. Vera commented that if a volunteer wanted to see a soldier outside of the events, she wrote her telephone number on a piece of paper and hid it inside a sandwich which she then gave to the soldier.

We also met a Polish man who spoke of the German invasion of his homeland. The Germans evicted his family and used the house to quarter soldiers. They killed his family and sent him to work in a slave labor camp. As the war progressed, the Nazis transferred him to work in a hospital where he had a little more freedom. The Allies slowly advanced and began to surround Germany. The Germans looked to dispose of the evidence of their atrocities. The prisoner met a Catholic priest who hid him and others in the church basement until the war ended. He made his way to the United States where he somehow reached out to a girl also hid by the priest. She later became his wife.

On a different outing to an assisted living facility for interviews, I took a group of students, one of which had a learning disability and sometimes had difficulty socializing with her peers. She interviewed a veteran and his wife who quickly became her adopted grandparents. She maintained a relationship with them for a long time after that initial interview. She developed confidence and really progressed due to her closeness with the elderly couple.

I caught a bug. I had to keep this going, learning as much as I could from those that directly experienced this incredible period in history and also making sure my students participated in this limited time opportunity. We interviewed other veterans at another facility and then the activity coordinator provided transportation for a whole group of veterans to speak to multiple classes at our high school. My students again typed up the interviews and we made copies of the videos of the interviews. Then students presented the veterans with special certificates of appreciation for their participation in the project as well as a copy of the video.

After a hiatus of five years due to my coaching and graduate school obligations, I started up again. This time around, finding veterans proved to be much more challenging. The average age of World War II veterans was obviously increasing. Fewer veterans were willing and able to meet with students whom the aging war heroes viewed as intimidating and uninterested in what they experienced over six decades ago.

I randomly called an old friend who recently had joined the Roswell Rotary Club. She mentioned something about an honor flight to Washington, D.C. It involved a trip taking one hundred World War II veterans to the nation's capitol to see their memorial before it was too late. I begged her to allow me to go on the trip. Everybody from Rotarians, community members, and relatives of veterans wanted to go but somehow I was chosen. I was a guardian (helper) to three veterans, one that I actually knew. He had spoken to my students the previous fall. To say it was a trip of a lifetime is an understatement. I met veterans and heard experiences I will never, ever forget. I forged friendships that exist today and have mourned the deaths of an ever increasing number of veterans. Since that first trip in the spring of 2008, I have been lucky enough to participate in three additional Honor Flights. The veterans experienced the local fire department saluting the caravan of busses with ladders that met over the road with an American flag draped down, and a police escort enabling us to speed through red lights. The police stopped traffic on the highway allowing the caravan to stay together all the way taking us to the exact gate at the airport where the veteran's experienced "modified" security. An honor guard of flag waving motorcycles and trucks accompanied the caravan to the airport and joined the veterans at the airport terminal. In Washington, D.C., the airline employees made an all call across the airport asking for everyone to congregate at the gate to greet the arriving heroes. The veterans departed the aircraft to the cheers of hundreds of admirers waving flags and shaking hands saying, "Thank you for your service."

During the second trip, local school children greeted the veterans with handwritten letters of thanks and praise. Another police escort enabled the caravan to easily maneuver through the streets to the World War II Memorial where decades of old memories resurfaced in aging minds. Passersby greeted the veterans and asked where the veterans served during the war.

Senators and Congressman took time out of their busy schedules to meet and greet the veterans from their home state and district. Setting off to the Lincoln, Vietnam, and Korean War Memorials, the veterans seemed to have more energy than their much younger helpers. At our final stop, the changing of the guard at Arlington National Cemetery, the war heroes stared in awe. Back at Reagan National Airport, bands greeted the veterans before their return trip to Atlanta. Tired veterans chatted like teenagers after an incredible one day journey.

My quest to find additional veterans to interview continued. I interviewed twenty or thirty veterans when someone suggested that I write a book compiling all these experiences. I said in reply that I wanted to interview more veterans and then maybe I would write a book. One day I read an article about an Honor Flight that operated out of Fayette County, Georgia. The article mentioned that one of the veterans on the trip was part of the crew of a B-17 Flying Fortress shot down over Austria. He became a prisoner of war for thirteen months. I called him and set up an interview. During my time with him I commented that his story should make up a part of my book. He said, "I have enough stories to make up an entire book! Will you write one about my experiences?" I simply said, "Sure I will."

A Life Anything But Ordinary

One
The Middle of the Dustbowl

Marvin Russell came close to death on multiple occasions. When his mind replays past events and how he successfully came through them, he is convinced, "I guess God has kept me around for a reason." Could God's reason be that Marvin Russell's story needed to be told? His story is one of hard work and perseverance, as well as personal and family tragedy. The Russell family lived and farmed at a time when much of the Great Plains became a dust bowl in the midst of the Great Depression.

Marvin's story began on February 27, 1922, in rural central Kansas in the small town of Galva with a population of about four hundred people. Marvin was born six weeks prematurely, weighing only five and half pounds. His mother delivered prior to the doctor's arrival at their country home. Because of his size, the doctor gave his parents no hope for his survival. Even at that early age, God had other plans for Marvin. About three months after he was born, his grandparents and their younger grandchildren decided to take an extended vacation to Arizona, but decided to stop by to "take their last look at the little fellow." Marvin's struggles did not end there. At the age of six months he contracted mumps, and again at the age of five years, and then again at age thirty-seven.

Marvin's family farmed two hundred and sixty acres of Kansas prairie growing mainly crops such as wheat, corn and oats, as well as alfalfa for the animals. They milked eight cows, raised two hundred chickens as well as a few hogs. Marvin said, "I can remember selling eggs for thirteen cents a dozen and butter fat for twenty-nine cents per pound." This was also in the days when gasoline cost eleven cents a gallon and tractor fuel nine cents a gallon.

During the Great Depression, the Russells fared better than many families since they grew and produced most of the food they needed. Since Marvin was the second child, he rarely if ever received new clothes, rather given his older brother's hand-me-downs instead. "When I was in the third or fourth grade," he remembered, "I had worn out overalls, but my brother always had new ones on. He received a new pair every year and the next year they were mine." During this time, Marvin attended school in a one room schoolhouse, maybe with thirty-two or thirty-three students total, with one teacher teaching eight grades. He lived about one and a half miles from school.

One beautiful day, the sun shining brightly, a huge black cloud appeared on the horizon, moving rapidly in the direction of the schoolhouse Marvin attended. This was before electricity in rural Kansas. The teacher lit lanterns which did little to help visibility because of all the dust in the air. Since there would be no learning that day, the teacher sent the children home unescorted, to face the unbearable dust. Marvin and the other children felt their way home, staying as far over to the side of the road. They worried about approaching vehicles whose drivers lacked the visibility to see the walking children. They could not see the cars until they appeared just in front or behind them. Luckily, only one car drove by on the walk home from school that day. The car stopped, and the men talked to Marvin and his classmates, but they didn't have room to give them a ride. Fortunately, the children all made it home safely that day.

When Marvin was nine or ten years old, he and his

Lily School was organized April 5, 1875, and was l. miles west on Highway 56 and 3 miles north in Canton T. Lily was consolidated April 22, 1955, with United Cente

Lily Teachers

1881 - H. M. Anderson; 1883 - D. B. Russel, Florence 1890 - H. E. Fenwick; 1891 - Myrtle Brown; 1892 - C. Mar. - Myrtle Coons; 1894 - Sammie Hartouft; 1895 - Herm: 1896-97 - Eva Griswold; 1898 - Maud Powers; 1899 - 1 Elliott; 1900 - Sophia Sandberg; 1901 - Cynthia Gettys; -Maude Way; 1904-06 - Willie Lovett; 1907 - Mable Eva -M. D. Landes; 1909 - Minnie Flook; 1901 - Carl Holm

Lily School, 1931 - Louie Phillipi, .. Cunningham, Yunietta Russell, C Cunningham, Theresia Schmidt, Leota Cunningham, ___, Chester Giesel, Wiederstein, Marvin Russell, Ethena Phillipi, ___, Arlen Cunningham, Malinda Wedel, , Delton Russell, , Verna Wedel, Clidy Wedel, Colby, Milton Wiederstein, Clarence Delay, Arnie Johnson.

neighbor, Arnie Johnson, played in the barn hayloft. Marvin climbed a ladder to the peak of the roof looking for a bird's nest and fell to the ground floor (probably twenty-five feet). He landed on his back with his arms under him to break the fall, breaking both wrists. Again, God intervened as a fall of this magnitude could have resulted in a much more serious injury. When Arnie brought him home, he suffered from unbearable pain. Going to the doctor in those days was not a common practice, so his parents decided against it. One of the first things he asked his mother was, "Do I have to milk the cows tonight?" It was about six weeks before he was able to complete that chore again.

Two
College Bound?

Not long after the end of the First World War, Benito
Mussolini assumed control of Italy desiring to build a modern
Roman Empire. Japan's imperial ruler, Hirohito, as well as its
militarist leaders, sought to extend its control and create the
Greater East Asia Co-Prosperity Sphere. To accomplish that
end, Japan needed natural resources, which it found in
neighboring Manchuria. In the early 1930s, Germany's aging
president, Paul von Hindenburg, became convinced by advisors
that a potentially dangerous National Socialist leader, Adolf
Hitler could be more easily controlled as Chancellor. Not long
after, the president died, leaving Adolf Hitler to use the rule by

decree provision in the Weimar Constitution to suspend the German Parliament, the Reichstag, and assume full control over Germany. Hitler became the Fuhrer and soon after sought to cleanse the population of so called undesirables and unite the true Germanic Aryans of Europe. Shortly after assuming power, Hitler began the persecution of Jewish Germans by passing the Nuremburg laws, basically compelling them to initially endure similar conditions to African Americans during the era of Jim Crow. As the 1930s progressed, so did the level of persecution of the Jews and others. The question many pondered was, to what level did Americans and others realize the extent of Hitler's actions?

Hitler was well known to Marvin and was the center of the topic of conversation just about everywhere. Referring to Hitler and Mussolini, Marvin said, "They were the worst in the world, and if we let them keep going they would get rid of all of us, it was only a matter of time." Though mainstream television did not make its way into American homes until the 1950s, families often spent evenings and other free time listening to the popular shows of the era and of course the news on the radio.

Marvin graduated from high school in 1940 and dreamed of attending college. Upon informing his folks of such a dream, his father replied, "You can go, but I am not sending you." His

The Russell children before the war
Courtesy of Marvin Russell

The Russell's new tractor participating in a local parade
Courtesy of Marvin Russell

parents had six children and thus said, "By the time I get through sending all of you, it will have cost me six thousand dollars." Marvin asked his father if he would at least take him to Pittsburg, Kansas to see the college. They agreed and upon arriving, his father drove right up to the main building. Marvin astutely marched into the president's office which was in Russ Hall. Marvin declared to the secretary, "I would like to talk to the president." The secretary replied, "Just a minute, I'll get him for you." President Brandenburg then came out and said, "What can I do for you?" Marvin replied, "I want to go to college, but all I have is fifty-five dollars." The aging president chuckled and replied, "Fifty-five dollars won't get you through college." Marvin was insistent and mentioned he realized that fact, so he would need a job as well. The president responded, "We can help you out with that." There it happened, Marvin Russell was enrolled in college!

The first day Marvin was in Chemistry class, and the name "Marvin Russell, report to the Dean of Men" was broadcast over the public address system. Marvin reacted by thinking, "I couldn't imagine what might happen. I've already gotten in trouble!" Marvin reported to the Dean of Men's office where he was told about a job at a restaurant twenty-seven blocks away. Since it was quite a walk, he needed a bicycle to get to work. The job entailed washing windows, floors, dishes, and any other odd jobs that needed completion. It paid one dollar and twenty-five cents a week, plus one meal a day. Marvin still remembers the Thursday meal and recalls, "I still think that on Thursdays when we had Swiss steak, it was the best Swiss steak that I've ever eaten. I would like to have some more of it!" The weekly salary was not getting Marvin very far. A short time later, Marvin was again called to the Dean of Men's office. Another job was offered. The second job required Marvin to sweep every classroom on the north half of the second floor of Russ Hall every day and on Saturdays he had to scrub the floors and marble stairs, wash the blackboards, and dust erasers. For this second job, Marvin earned forty dollars per month. While reminiscing, Marvin leaned his head back in his chair and sighed before commenting, "I thought I'd struck gold!"

Marvin made it through his first year of college and planned on going back for a second. However, the war was getting closer. Germany had invaded Poland on December 1, 1939, drawing the United Kingdom, as well as the British Empire, and France into the war. Japan brought French Indochina into its sphere of influence in September, 1940. Marvin's older brother, Delton, had not gone to college but instead answered a newspaper advertisement placed by the

Swallow Aircraft Company about an aircraft inspection and riveting school in Wichita, Kansas. A representative of the company travelled to their home and Delton signed up for the seven week riveting course. The representative then asked Marvin what his future plans entailed. Since Marvin had already attended one year of college, he was told he was just the man they were looking for to be an inspector. Marvin decided to take the sixteen week inspection course.

On December 7, 1941, Marvin was home on the farm helping his father fill the silo when his mother ran out to inform them that the Japanese had bombed Pearl Harbor. Due to this fateful news, Marvin did not get the chance to finish the inspection course. In between Christmas and New Years, R.C. Brown, formerly Chief Inspector at Beech Aircraft Corporation and instructor at Swallow Aircraft Company obtained a position at Emerson Electric Company. He called to ask Marvin to come and work for him. Marvin took the job as a gauge inspector and worked for about ten months.

Emerson Electric Company, founded in 1890, was called upon by the United States Ordinance Department in 1940 to produce brass shell casings, finally producing over ten million by war's end. The company also produced gun turrets, particularly the "model 127" mounted in the nose of the B-24 bomber. 2

There were seven or so men that were hired from the inspection school in Wichita that went to work for Emerson Electric Company. After returning home one night, Marvin saw a note from one of the men indicating he wanted to join the service. Rather than enlisting individually, the men decided to do so as a group with hopes of staying together. Marvin knew one day his draft number would be called so going together with guys he knew was a much better alternative. When asked why he chose the Army Air Corps, Marvin replied, "I have no idea."

Three
East and West I Go!

In October 1942, prior to Marvin's enlistment in the
Army Air Corps, he explained that Emerson Electric Company
bought gauges from an outside vendor. All the paperwork
concerning the purchases went through his office. Marvin
worked in the tool inspection department and received the
gauges from the shipping department. Mr. Fleming, Marvin's
boss, made a habit of coming to Marvin's department taking
whatever gauges he wanted for his own use. One particular
Sunday, Marvin was working when a man wearing an office
badge loitered around the entrance to the office and waited for
Marvin to lock up. The man with the badge said "Mr. Russell,

you've got to come with me. First of all, go to the other end of the building and clock out. I'll meet you up here at the door going to guard headquarters." The man escorted Marvin to a room where he was introduced to Mr. Hines, who was an agent with the Federal Bureau of Investigation. Two hours of questioning led to the opening of a case that also involved two of Marvin's co workers. The F.B.I. agent informed Marvin that Mr. Fleming and Mr. Kirkpatrick had a system worked out where one would clock in for both of them. The other performed the same favors on the later shift, earning both of them many extra hours of pay. On one of these days, Fleming was out horseback riding and broke his arm while on the clock. In spite of Marvin finding himself in the middle of this situation, he considered Mr. Hines the "finest man I ever spoke with." Mr. Hines then informed Marvin that he was not permitted to go into the service at that time due to the open investigation involving Marvin's coworkers. He said they would make all the arrangements for Marvin and he could go later when the case was settled. A couple of days later, the agent changed his mind and said that Marvin could indeed go into the service, but would have to come back for the trial.

Marvin took his basic training at Midland Air Base in west-central Texas half way between Midland and Odessa.

Official military photograph, courtesy of Marvin
Russell

Midland Air Base began as Sloan Field and initially provided a
location that offered flight training and a civilian airfield. It
became an Army Airways Station in 1930 and nine years later
under the Works Progress Administration, runways were
improved and a year later runway lights installed. After the fall
of France in 1940, the airfield became a training base for the
Army Flying Training Program. In the summer of 1941, the

United States Government leased the airfield for a dollar a year whereupon they improved the base. The base and Army Air Corps facility was nicknamed Bombardier College and designated Air Corps Advanced Twin Engine and Bombardier Training Center. On September 26, 1942, the Army renamed the base yet again to Army Air Forces Bombardier School. Initial training began on February 6, 1942. By war's end, 6,627 bombardiers were trained at the base. Marvin was among them, joining on November 2, 1942. 3

One day during practice drills, a 2nd lieutenant informed Marvin that Captain Baker wanted to see him for a telephone call. It was Mr. Hines, the F.B.I. agent handling the case against Mr. Fleming and Mr. Kirkpatick. He said they were in court that day. Mr. Hines advised Marvin that he should be prepared to answer questions from lawyers that would be broadcast over the loudspeaker in the courtroom. A few days later they sent him a copy of the St. Louis Post Dispatch with a picture of Mr. Fleming and Mr. Kirkpatrick and under it an article saying that they had received ten years in prison and faced a fine of $10,000 each.

Four
Basic Training

Basic training at Midland Air Base began on November 2, 1942, and ended December 28 of that year. Training was cut short due to the need to move soldiers through basic and into various positions in the armed forces. The Army Air Corps needed Marvin in Lincoln, Nebraska. Early one morning, a list was posted on the bulletin board containing the names of fifty men to be shipped to Kelly Field in San Antonio, Texas. The list was cut to twenty-five men and Marvin remained as the only one from his original group that enlisted together chosen to go.

Kelly Field traces its history back to 1916 as the South San Antonio Aviation Camp and is the oldest air base currently

in operation. It was renamed Camp Kelly and then again Kelly Field in 1917. Kelly Field was named after Lieutenant George E.M. Kelly who died in 1911 while piloting a military aircraft. He was the first such casualty. It was established to expand the Aviation Flying Section of the United States Army Signal Corps. Most of the airmen that flew during the First World War came through Kelly Field for instruction or processing. 4 Between the world wars, the future of what became known as the Air Force was a point of controversy. The question at hand was whether the War Department should integrate the air component of the military with the army or have it remain as a separate entity of the other branches of the United States Armed Forces. Investment in Kelly Field increased tremendously just prior to the Second World War. Between 1940 and 1943 construction projects included buildings that provided instruction, administration, airplane repair, supply, and barracks. It is well known that a tremendous number of women entered the work force during the war years and Kelly Field provided employment to many who were referred to as "Kelly Katies." 5

From Midland Air Base, Marvin was processed and later sent to Airplane Mechanics School in Lincoln Nebraska. The war effort in Lincoln was featured in the July 4, 1943 edition of the *Sunday World-Herald Magazine:*

Nearly 30 thousand fighter-mechanics have been graduated from the Army Air Forces' Technical Training Command's airplane Mechanics school at the Army Air Base at Lincoln, Neb., since June of 1942, when the first students arrived. Time and again, praise and condemnation of his graduates have come back to Brig. Gen. Early F. W. Duncan, commanding general of the base, from the factories where men have been sent

for advance training and from the fighting fronts where
these men are proving their
'know how.'

Glamour of the air forces is usually
consigned to flight personnel, but
the fact is, it takes seven ground crew
men to keep even pursuit ships in flying
shape. Although the fighter-mechanics
are little known or generally appreciated,
it is their responsibility to maintain the
power, accuracy and deadliness of each
plane in the air forces' rapidly expanding
armada. Though short on glamour, these
men are long on what it takes to keep 'em
flying. . . .

To train men in maintenance, the base's
technical school is open 24 hours each day.
Classrooms and hangars are in operation day
and night; work never ceases around the clock,
seven days a week. Upon the completion of
the five-month course, a soldier-technician is
skilled, ready for assignment to one of the
army's numerous air bases or installations.
At that time, some technicians are selected
for advanced training, and sent to an airplane
factory for additional specialized training.

During the five-month training period, the
fighter-mechanics study every phase of the
nation's fastest pursuit ships. At first they
become familiar with the fundamental tools,

used in maintaining such aircraft progressing
through fuselage construction, materials used in
maintenance, and complete
instruction in the engines of these planes.
In the final part of his training each student
is schooled in actual combat training,
working under simulated war zone conditions
at the new testing phase of instruction at
the recently activated field test division, at
Ashland, Neb. 6

Training lasted five months and culminated on May 1,
1943, when Marvin was transferred to Inglewood, California for
B-25 training at the North American Aviation Plant. He then
went to Tyndall Field, located near Panama City, Florida for six
weeks of gunnery training. Afterwards, Marvin was assigned to
a B-17 Flying Fortress crew in Salt Lake City, Utah. Later, the
crew became part of the 407th Squadron of the 92nd Bomb
Group of the Eight Air Force.

Then it was off to Ephrata, Washington for bomb
training. Ephrata Army Air Base was used extensively for heavy
bomber training. 7 Marvin's crew dropped one hundred pound
bombs and practiced hitting their targets which Marvin
explained, "lit up on the ground, flying at night." Marvin's job
as engineer and top turret gunner was to take the pins out of the
bombs so that when they dropped they would detonate. On one

particular mission, Marvin crossed the catwalk to the bomb bay to remove the pins. The bombardier was not supposed to open it until the pins were removed. For some reason, on this occasion, he started to open the doors prematurely. A funny experience followed: "That would have been alright but there's a universal joint in each side that went straight across and my pants leg caught on the universal. It started rolling up on there all the way up to the top, pulling them apart which pulled my pants off!!" The pilot, Lt. John C Campbell, pulled him out, and when they landed, he instructed Marvin to walk around the hangar to get to his barracks to avoid being seen by officers of higher rank for fear they would question why he was without pants!

From Ephrata, Marvin was sent to Eugene, Oregon for more training. There, for a week to ten days, Marvin participated in missions every day. When asked what the purpose was for going to Eugene, Marvin answered, "I wish you wouldn't ask that because I don't know. I don't know why we were there! We didn't do anything there that we didn't do at Ephrata."

It was at this time that Marvin received his one and only delay-in-route during his time in the service. His orders directed him to travel to Avon Park, Florida with a weeklong furlough to home in Kansas. "I remember telling my folks, this will be the last time I'll ever be here." Marvin explained to his parents that out of all the bombers that embarked out of England, many did not complete their missions. He attempted not to dwell on the fate of his comrades, but faced the viability of potential survivors. There were so many that were reported as either killed or missing in action. Marvin's father, a veteran of the First World War, suddenly became keenly aware of the dangers his son faced.

While on the delay-in-route at home, Marvin's brother Delton planned to marry and asked Marvin to stand up as his best man. Prior to the wedding, Marvin had never met the bridesmaid, Lois, but definitely became impressed by her beauty. They ultimately wed on November 24, 1945, shortly after his discharge from the Army Air Corps.

After the delay-in-route ended, Marvin headed to Avon Park, located in South Central Florida in order to conduct further missions similar to those conducted in Ephrata, Washington. Avon Park Air Field was a training facility for B-17 crews for air to ground target practice. There, Marvin trained with one hundred pound bombs. 8 One day, his superior officer told him the crew would not be dropping real bombs since evidently there was a shortage.

Five
First Rendezvous with Death

The flight crew was told to take a trip somewhere, anywhere they wanted to go. It was a nice day with a clear blue sky and the pilot said, "How about we go to Atlanta?" Everybody agreed so they started out flying toward Atlanta. Upon arriving at the Georgia-Florida line, the sky clouded over which forced the crew to rely increasingly on instruments rather than visual signs to determine their height and location. No one had reset the altimeter. The altitude at Avon Park is ten feet, while in Atlanta the altitude is above 1,000 feet. The crew relied on instruments at about three thousand feet and decided to take a look at Atlanta. The aircraft descended through the clouds surrounding Atlanta and ultimately realized they were engulfed by fog around the Austell area. Marvin stood immediately behind the pilot, looking out the window when the crew lost all visibility.

Immediately in front of the approaching aircraft was a two story house where Marvin saw a woman running as fast as she could toward that house. The plane suddenly jolted and they realized that they had lost a wing from the number one engine on out. Since the altimeter had not been reset, the aircraft flew more than one thousand feet lower than expected and resulted in colliding with a tree. The problem the crew now faced is how to fly a one winged plane? The pilot gave it full throttle and asked, "Where can we land?"

Unbelievably, the aircraft stayed in the air. Marvin looked out toward the wing and saw that the aileron protruded a foot past where the wing broke off. "If that would have come out we would have gone down." They decided to land at the nearest base, having no idea of where they were but since they could go on so they headed toward Columbus, Georgia. How could they fly without a wing? Marvin answered, "On a wing and a prayer!"

They rapidly approached the airfield but the pilot had not yet made contact with the tower and the crew had no idea where they were. They came in on the air pattern and sitting on the runway were two single engine AT-6 training aircraft ready for takeoff. As they prepared to land, the pilot saw the aircraft and gave it full throttle, barely making it up over the top of them, with hopes of going around and landing behind where the airplanes were parked. When they circled around again, Marvin saw that the planes were moved off into the grass, unprotected. The tower could not contact Marvin's airplane nor could they contact the tower as they were not on the right frequency. Unbelievably, they made it onto the ground. The fact that Marvin and the crew survived is a miracle as the airplane should have crashed.

Marvin was the first of his crew off the airplane and quickly encountered a General who saluted him. Marvin, an enlisted man, informed the General that he was neither the pilot nor an officer and that the man he sought was still on the plane. The General said, "I want you and the pilot to come with me." Marvin and the pilot, Lt. Campbell, rode with the General in his staff car to his orderly room. The General called the base at Avon Park, Florida, and told them he had one of their planes with only one wing and its crew. The next thing he said was, "They hit a tree!" After notifying the base, the General, the Pilot, and Marvin returned to the one-winged plane. Marvin wanted to see where the wing had broken off. They wheeled over a moveable ladder so he could climb up. He found a piece of the tree embedded in the engine mount. It was only a short time before another airplane was sent from Avon Park to pick up the crew.

At this point in the interview, Marvin asked if he could be excused. I moved out of the way and he walked into the other room and brought back a piece of wood that he said had blackened over the years. It was the piece of wood from the tree the airplane had hit that had gotten stuck in the wing. Later on, when Marvin and the crew were reported missing in action, the military sent the piece of wood as well as the rest of his personal possessions home to Kansas. When Marvin made it home, his folks asked, "What is that little piece of wood that you got?" He explained the adventurous situation of how it came to be.

Six
Off to an Unknown World

From Avon Park, Marvin and his crew flew to Savannah,
Georgia for about two weeks. From there, the crew picked up a
new B-17 in order to fly over to the United Kingdom. On New
Years Eve, 1943 the crew departed Savannah via the southern
route which consisted of stopping or refueling in Puerto Rico,
Atkinson Field in British Guiana, Natal, Brazil in South
America, to Dakar, Senegal in French West Africa and then
progressing to Scotland. When the crew arrived in Puerto Rico
they realized that the B-17 had a Tokyo valve that was not
working properly. Each wing possessed an extra fuel tank with a
valve that switched from the main fuel tank to the spare tanks

when the airplane ran low on fuel. Apparently, the crew that flew the airplane from the factory near Seattle did not recognize the problem. Marvin was the first to identify the malfunction and a new valve was required before the crew could move on. The part had to be ordered from the plant in Seattle and then flown to meet the airplane. The new part met the crew and airplane in British Guiana whereupon the assistant engineer and Marvin changed out the valve.

One of Marvin's favorite memories of being in British Guiana were the bananas. For twenty-five cents the locals brought him all he could eat, which allowed Marvin the luxury of gorging himself on the native treat.

Though the northern route appears shorter than the southern route, it actually was safer. A friend of Marvin's that he had gone to school with deployed via airplane two to three months prior and went down over Iceland. The plane experienced problems and had to land. Once on the ground, the crew walked until they could not proceed any further. They walked until the ice had broken open and his friend went down to the bottom. Marvin remarked, "We haven't heard from him since."

It was such a long distance to travel that by the time they hit the runway in Dakar, they were completely out of fuel. On the route from Dakar to Scotland, the B-17 flew around the Mediterranean Sea and saw a convoy of ships. One of the ships flashed its light communicating in Morse code. The co-pilot flashed back questioning, were they friend or foe? Nothing was fired up at them so they were in the clear. They landed in Scotland and trained in 'The Wash,' on the east coast of England, where the men undertook gunnery practice.

After about two weeks, they headed to London for a couple days for rest and relaxation. They hoped to tour the town and possibly take in a show. The largest United Service Organization outfit outside the United States was located in London. There they offered entertainment and shows for G.I.'s traveling through London. Marvin has absolutely the funniest laugh, it really is contagious. When asked about his time in London, Marvin leaned his head back and laughed and laughed. I said, "Uh oh, there must be a story! You must have had some great times in London!" Marvin proceeded to explain that one night after supper as he and the crew's waistgunner walked down the street, they were approached by an English woman wearing nothing but a fur coat. She flung open her coat and propostioned, "What do you think Yanks?" Due to most young British men serving abroad, single ladies were eager to meet the American newcomers. Older Brits often described the American servicemen as, "overpaid, oversexed, and over here."

By this time, Germany began deploying the V-2 rockets. While in London, Marvin and the crew favored a certain breakfast establishment. While taking in some pints one evening, the pub was bombed by the rockets. They ran out onto the street and glass was blown clear over everything. They reluctantly walked back to the place where they were staying and were relieved to find it was still standing. The next day, the men happened to walk by the restaurant that they had eaten breakfast the day before and found it totally destroyed. On the way back to the hotel, Marvin walked by the remnants of buildings mostly destroyed when he heard someone hollering. When they arrived, rescue personnel worked to free the man from the rubble of the building. It was then they realized it was a G.I. who had been there since the bombing the night before. He screamed and yelled until they got him loose yet unfortunately, after his rescue, he died.

On March 1, 1944, Marvin and the crew arrived at their new base, Royal Air Force Base Podington near Wellingborough, England. RAF Podington, constructed between 1940 and 1941 was transferred over to the United States Army Air Corps in 1942. The Eighth Air Force was sent to the United Kingdom to expedite the Allied bombing campaign. Without

9

10. B-17 Flying Fortresses on a bombing mission

knowing it at the time, Marvin was part of the longest continuous battle of the Second World War. 11 A couple of days after arriving, Marvin and his crew began participating in daylight missions over Nazi Germany.

American bombing missions almost always occurred during the daytime which resulted in far higher accuracy than nighttime bombing but also resulted in higher casualty rates for pilots. Bombardiers utilized the Norden Bombsight which greatly assisted in bombing accuracy. At the peak of the war, 1,300,000 men fought in air combat roles flying some 28,000 aircraft. American men lost in action totaled 79,265 and British 79,281. It is important to note that although some American pilots volunteered to fly with the Royal Air Force to defend against Luftwaffe attacks during the Battle of Britain, American forces were not truly vested until late 1941. Thus, these statistics point to the extreme danger American crews endured during daylight missions. 12

American Army Air crews hit the cities of Kassel, Hamm, Swineford, Berlin, and Frankfort, located on the Rhine River. Kassel became the home to companies such as Henschel & Son that produced war equipment, specifically Tiger and Panzer tanks, as well as various types of aircraft for the Luftwaffe making it a target for allied bombing. 13 Allied bombing began on October 22, 1943, that resulted in destruction of most of the inner city. Besides dropping bombs on Kassel, they also dropped newspapers printed in German containing American propaganda similar to radio broadcasters Axis Sally and Tokyo Rose. Marvin's squadron participated in what became his final mission on April 24, 1944, that set out to destroy a Luftwaffe aerodrome or airfield. Later, bombing raids resulted in great destruction of residential and industrial sites, specifically seventy percent and sixty-five percent respectively. 14

During every mission, Marvin thought about the effect Allied bombing had on civilians. He said, "You couldn't help but think about it." He hated that their bombing killed innocent people but realized that taking out industrial and military targets hastened the end to the war and far fewer people might be killed in the long run.

Due to its proximity to Germany's industrial Ruhr and its importance as a marshalling yard as well as a transportation hub of war material and steel, Hamm became a target after Kassel. Germany anticipated Allied bombing and prepared Hamm with extensive anti-aircraft flak protection. 15 Flak abbreviated from the German word, Fliegerabwehrkanone means anti-aircraft gun. Flak from German canons, directed at approaching airplanes exploded and fragments flew in all directions. The fragments were capable of penetrating the outer skin of the aircraft. On their first mission, the crew counted one hundred and five holes in the aircraft that resulted from flak. Hamm was home to an important railroad yard as well as war production facilities. American bombers reduced much of Hamm to rubble, crippling Germany's war making capability. Next was Frankfurt, home to important chemical producer IG Farben, maker of Zyklon B, used in the gas chambers in concentration camps all over Nazi occupied Europe. Frankfurt also possessed a very important rail yard and large amounts of coal. Marvin recalled that after his squadron bombed the rail yard, the Germans had it operational with one track cleared within twenty-four hours. "I know that because I was there. I saw it. I saw all those freight cars and engines lying out there on their sides."

Seven
The End of Me

On the morning of what became Marvin's final mission, the men received a briefing on what to do should they get shot down. As they were shown a map of Europe, they were told that if they got shot down "up here," they should attempt to get to Denmark, where they could get help and make their way back to England. Even though the Danish were under Nazi control following the fall of Poland in September, 1939, the Germans allowed them a degree of autonomy since Denmark hardly resisted German takeover. It is well known that the Danish underground worked to help nearly all of its Jewish citizens' escape to neutral Sweden often via fishing boats. If the men were forced to bail out "down here" meaning at a point on the map of Southern France, they were briefed to search for a member of the resistance to guide them across the Pyrenees Mountains and get them to Spain or Portugal. Each Nazi occupied country possessed civilians loyal to the cause of liberation from the Germans that became part of resistance movements. They acted selflessly and often took great risks to undermine German rule. The consequence for assisting the Allies was death or internment at one of many concentration camps.

The Germans divided France into two sections. The northern section was under direct control of the Nazis where as many as three million men were enslaved to work building Hitler's Atlantic Wall. Hitler anticipated a future Allied invasion of his "fortress Europe" and following the fall of France in 1940, began the long process of constructing the two thousand mile long coastline defense. The southern part of France with its capital at Vichy was under the leadership of Marshall Petain, and while having the allusion of independence really operated in collaboration with the Germans.

The briefing continued with information involving a target in the town of Oberpfaffenhofen, Germany which housed a very important company. Allied intelligence learned of a wide

Marvin Russell with his crew, second from the right hand side
Courtesy of Marvin Russell

range of military aircraft production at the Dornier AC Company in the town of Oberpfaffenhofen. This became Marvin's bomb crew's next target. The crew on this mission consisted of the pilot, Earl Howard, chosen as a replacement for the regular pilot, John C. Campbell, who could not accompany the crew on this mission. The others included the co-pilot, Glenn Filbirth; the bombardier, Eugene McGinn; the navigator Bill, LaGard; the radio operator, Joe Oklak; one of the waist gunners, Levi Burns; the other waist gunner, Hubert Metlock; the ball turret gunner, Ralph Mercheson; and the tail gunner, Victor Wells.

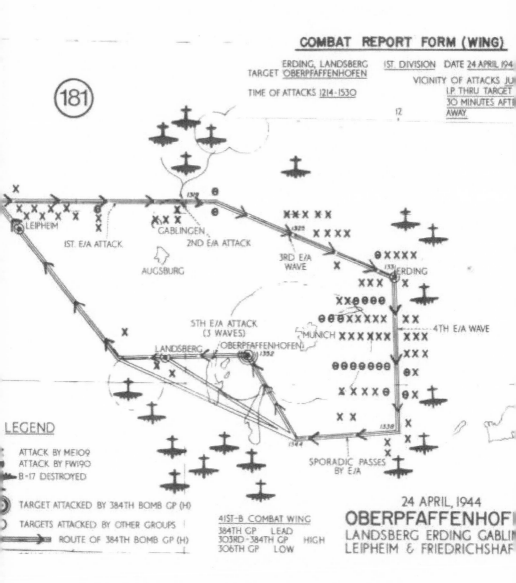

16. Marvin's flight plan for their mission over Oberphaffenhofen, Germany...his final mission.

During this mission, the squadron flew with P-38 fighter escorts, but not all the way to Germany and back due to their limited fuel capacity. On Marvin's seventh mission, which took place April 24, 1944, the squadron departed the air base at 0600 hours with orders to hit their targets at 1300 hours. They flew against a strong head wind making it take longer to reach the target. The pilot was new to Marvin's crew having never flown on a bombing mission before. He asked a lot of questions that seasoned pilots would not ask. He was on his first mission and the B-17 crew's seventh. The crew's regular pilot flew two days later on a mission to Hamm, Germany but his plane went down due to Hamm's extensive flak batteries in operation. The pilot, Lt. Campbell, did not survive.

Before they neared their targets, the P-38 fighter escort planes ran low on fuel, forcing them to return to their base. At approximately the same time, P-51s were scheduled to replace the P-38s as escorts. Marvin received word over the radio that fighters were seen at nine o'clock level. They were too far away to tell if they were friend or foe. But when they appeared in range, a crew member called out, "Fighters at 12 o'clock high." It was noted that the fighter planes were German Messerschmitt 109s and not American P-51 fighters. Soon, the German fighters were dead ahead of them, flying straight toward the American bombers. Marvin's B-17 was struck on the first pass and had to drop out of formation. Machine gun fire hit the number one engine, catching it on fire. Fire also erupted in the gas tank on the bomber's right hand side. From the top turret gunner position, Marvin could see fire spewing out from a small hole in the center of the right wing. The flame shot back eighteen to twenty inches. The pilot feathered the propeller on the number one engine extinguishing that fire. Feathering the propeller involves maneuvering the blade so that it is positioned parallel to the flow of air which reduces drag to the aircraft.

Before the pilot began the rapid descent in order to extinguish the fire in the wing, Marvin warned that diving was a possibility but there was a limit to how long they could dive due to the increased flight speed. While descending, Marvin looked and the air speed indicator went way past the peg. Marvin yelled, "Pull it out, pull it out, you'll break this plane in two!" The pilot started leveling the bomber when they began their ascent back up to the original altitude of 32,000 feet. The fire went from the small hole in the wing all the way back to the tail. When returned to their final climbing altitude, he said, "It's time to get out of here, its going to blow." The pilot replied, "I'll give the command." The crew bailed out at 32,000 feet.

B-17 Flying Fortresses have a ten person crew; the pilot

who obviously flies the plane but is also the overall commander, the co-pilot who is the backup pilot and is in charge of maneuvering the plane while on the ground, the flight engineer and top turret gunner who is also in charge of monitoring the status of the engines, the navigator who monitors the airplane position and direction, the bombardier who determines when and where to deploy the bombs, the radio operator who handles all communication, the ball turret gunner who protects the bomber from enemy fighter fire coming from below, two waist gunners that protect the plane from attack to the sides of the plane, and a tail gunner, located at the rear of the aircraft. 17

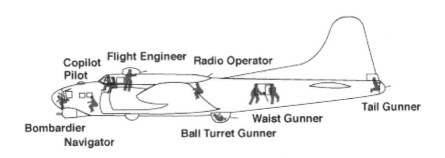

18. Crew positions of the B-17 Flying Fortress

Two escape doors existed on the B-17, the waist door in the back, and a hatch in the front. The waist gunners, the radio operator, the ball turret gunner and tail gunner all jumped out the waist door. The navigator, the bombardier, the pilot, co-pilot and Marvin, the flight engineer and top turret gunner went out the hatch underneath the pilot. Marvin geared up to jump after the bombardier who hesitated in the crouched down position. Marvin, knowing they could not waste time, gave the man some help and pushed him out of the plane. "He went out alright! I went right behind him."

The ball turret gunner position proved a dangerous one for two reasons. The ball turret gunner is responsible for manning two machine guns that when pointed straight forward, can catch a deploying parachute if the rip cord is pulled too soon. The other major issue that many ball turret gunners experienced dealt with electrical problems. Due to temperatures as low as minus fifty-two degrees at high altitudes, the crew had electrically heated suits. In the event of electricity failure, the ball turret gunner often froze to death. The ball turrets that dropped down beneath the airplane also rotated and if the electricity failed, the gunner became stuck. If the plane went down and the crew bailed, the ball turret gunners rarely made it out of the aircraft. Fortunately, the entire crew made it out of

Marvin's bomber.

Marvin's crew was among over fourteen hundred other bomber crews in B-17 aircraft that set out that day to destroy targets in the Munich area of southern Germany. Marvin's crew sought to take out an airplane parts factory in Oberpfaffenhofen, Germany at 1300 hours. They bailed out at around 32,000 feet near Lake Constance, Switzerland, high up over the Alps at 1245 hours, just fifteen minutes shy of reaching their destination. "It looked like it was raining parachutes," Marvin described as he looked all around him after jumping. There were fighters all around, approaching from every direction.

It was important that when airmen jumped that they did not pull the rip cord right away. For one reason, as mentioned, the parachute could get caught on the ball turret gunner's machine guns. Secondly, the lack of oxygen in the air at that altitude often resulted in suffocation if the airmen pulled the rip cord too soon. Also, a longer time period in free fall reduced exposure to enemy fighters. Instructions for the rip cord read, "Do not pull the rip cord until you can see the ground coming up." Free fall occurs at around one hundred nineteen miles an hour but when the rip cord is pulled and the parachute opens, it slows the airmen down to seventeen to eighteen miles an hour which in this situation, made them perfect targets for German fighters. Additionally it was cold, at least fifty degrees below zero. As Marvin descended in free fall, he passed countless parachutes from other bomber crews whose occupants pulled the rip cord too soon.

Lake Constance, partially fed by the Rhine River, lies between Germany, Switzerland, and Austria. Marvin pulled his rip cord late and as a result had less time to maneuver therefore landing in a pine tree. He fell to the ground and pulled off his Mae West life jacket and attempted to bury that along with his parachute to avoid detection by the Germans. Two to three minutes later, Marvin spotted three German civilians, armed with shotguns so he dropped the two items and dashed off in the opposite direction. It did not matter that these men were not members of the German military. If the Nazis learned that these civilians found an American airman and did not take him as a prisoner, they would have met their demise. The Germans split up, two going in the direction of where Marvin disposed of his Mae West and parachute. The other walked straight toward him. The two ended up finding his disposed of items, signaling an American flyer in the area. When the two Germans found the parachute and Mae West, they shouted, and the man who headed toward Marvin turned and went to join the first two.

Marvin did not find anyone from his flight crew but one

of the waist gunners did find the navigator. "Everybody was on his own. I was on the loose for five or six days." Marvin had his escape pack on him, which consisted of a map which he did not want the Germans to find, plus crackers and a compass. "I wasn't all that hungry though," Marvin said with a chuckle. Since it was April, much of the Alps were still covered in snow. Marvin learned later that the part of the crew that jumped after him landed in snow since the airplane continued to fly for a while. Marvin moved at night to avoid detection since Austria was under Nazi control since the *Anschluss,* in 1938. On two different occasions Marvin was forced to cross a stream. He waded across one and fell clear up to his waist which forced him to take off all his clothes, wring his pants out and dump the water out of his shoes once he made it to the other side. Marvin attempted to avoid detection by avoiding towns at all costs. If he saw a light on, he went the other way. He saw lights in what he thought was Switzerland but was told never to cross the Swiss border, considered the most heavily guarded border.

After walking a great distance, he found a triangular clearing of trees that measured approximately two hundred feet in each direction. Those that cleared the trees piled all the brush in the middle of the triangle. Marvin hoped to climb under that pile of brush and hide for the duration of the day. It rained all day long and Marvin learned soon enough that his hiding spot lay in a gully and "here came the water which meant I had to get out!" Marvin walked for a ways and found a railroad trestle and encountered two men on one side of it. They were Italian prisoners of war working on the trestle. He walked up and started talking to the men and although they spoke different languages, Marvin tried to communicate that he needed civilian clothing to escape. The two men took Marvin to a small house and pointed to a pair of overalls hanging on a hook. What he soon learned was that one of the men, rather than deciding to help Marvin, went to a guard to turn him in instead. "That was the end of me!"

Less than one week following the downing of Marvin's B-17, two soldiers from Smoky Hill Army Air Force Base, Salina, Kansas, drove to the family farm and reported Marvin's Missing In Action status. Four months passed before his family received a letter from the War Department advising that Marvin was a Prisoner of War. They provided information to the family of how to write to Marvin. Communication from a P.O.W. camp to the United States was a very slow process. The Red Cross provided form letters used by inmates to communicate with their families. The letters were censored and many parts were blacked out or omitted.

The letter on the following page is from Marvin's mother dated April 25, 1945, and is typical of those sent by the International Red Cross to and from P.O.W.s.

INSTRUCTIONS

MAIL TO EUROPE: WRITE VERY CLEARLY BETWEEN THE LINES OR TYPE OR PRINT IN BLOCK CAPITALS.

MAIL TO FAR EAST: LIMIT MAIL TO JAPAN TO 24 WORDS. TYPE OR BLOCK PRINT ONLY—DO NOT WRITE IN SCRIPT.

Remember that Legible Mail can be handled Faster

APRIL 25, 1945

Dear Marvin, I hope you are so far away from
Stalag 17B by the time this gets there that
you never even see it. Yesterday was uncle
Lucien's sale and they had a real nice day and
a big crowd. Things sold real well. The Grange
Ladies cleared around 50 dollars at the stand.
We got your personal belongings yesterday, I
didn't know just what to look for so don't
know if we got all we should have or not.
We have a real scandal around here now. If you
remember a while back I told you that Theresa
Schmidt had a baby and her husband (Archie
Phillis) has been overseas for 14 months. Well
she wrote and told him that Glen Asp is the
father to the baby. So Archie wrote back to
his folks and had them to start divorce
proceedings at once. I don't know if she
intends to make Glen Asp marry her or not. There
is a story out that she isn't sure who the Dad
may be, that it might be Ben Fortner or Kenny
Schultz. Now I don't know a thing about it.
She says it all happened because Bill Hager's
took her to dances in McPherson. A good excuse
isn't it? Virgil was up here to-day and he and
Dad made him a rack to put a 250 gallon gasoline
tank on for him to use while he is plowing.
We got the letter Monday that you wrote on
Feb 15, was so glad to get it. I don't see
why you got the cigarettes and not the other

CONTINUE ON REVERSE SIDE AT TOP PANEL

package as the other one was sent first. I
hope before now you have received several
the packages I have sent to you. The kids
getting all ready for their last day of s
day after to-morrow, they started on their
program to-day. I thought so much yesterd
about you being a P.O.W. for a year. It h
seemed like such a long year to us, waiti
and being able to do nothing. I pray it i

The letter from Marvin's mother reads:

INSTRUCTIONS
MAIL TO EUROPE: WRITE VERY CLEARLY BETWEEN
THE LINES OR TYPE OR PRINT IN
BLOCK CAPITALS.
MAIL TO FAR EAST: LIMIT MAIL TO JAPAN TO 24
WORDS. TYPE OR BLOCK PRINT
ONLY-DO NOT WRITE IN SCRIPT.
REMEMBER that LEGIBLE MAIL can be handled FASTER
April 25, 1945

Dear Marvin, I hope you are so far away from Stalag 17 B by the time this gets there that you never even see it. Yesterday was uncle Lucien's sale and they had a real nice day and a big crowd . Things sold real well. The Grange Ladies cleared around 50 dollars at the stand. We got your personal belongings yesterday, I didn't know just what to look for so don't know if we got all we should have or not. We have a real scandal around here now. If you remember a while back I told you that Theresa Schmidt had a baby and her husband (Archie Phillis) has been overseas for 14 months. Well she wrote and told him that Glen Asp is the father to the baby. So Archie wrote back to his folks and had them to start divorce proceedings at once. I don't know if she intends to make Glen Asp marry her or not. There is a story out that she isn't sure who the Dad may be. That it might be Ben Fortner or Kenny Schultz. Now I don't a thing about it. She says it all happened because Bill Hager's took to her to dances in McPherson. A good excuse isn't it? Virgil was up here to-day and he and Dad made him a rack to put a 250 gallon gasoline on for him to use while he is plowing. We got the letter Monday that you wrote on Feb 15, was so glad to get it. I don't see why you got the cigarettes and not the other package as the other one was sent first. I hope before now you have received several of the packages I have sent to you. The kids are all getting ready for there last day of school day after to-morrow, they started on their program to-day. I thought so much yesterday about you being a P.O.W. for a year. It has seemed like such a long year to me, waiting and being able to do nothing. I pray it is...(it appears the next line is blacked out).

Eight
Thirteen Months

The guard took Marvin to a large white two-story house on the hill nearby. There was an elderly lady with her hair in a knot along with nineteen pregnant girls living in that house. They were raising babies for Hitler. The elderly lady brought him some oatmeal and put it on the table and then put her index finger to her lips and shushed him. In that kitchen sat an old cupboard which had a secret compartment presumably to hide scarce and rationed goods. She reached in the back of it and brought out a little brown bag of sugar. The old woman brought out the sugar and spread some over the oatmeal. Just as quickly as she took out the bag, she replaced it in the secret compartment in the cabinet. Not long after Marvin arrived at this house, the constable from a nearby town came to take him away. He and Marvin started walking and crossed a bridge that crossed a good sized creek. Marvin suddenly realized that he still carried his escape pack, and knowing it would no longer be needed, he threw it in the water. The constable walked about fifteen or twenty feet in front of Marvin and he heard a splash and turned around to look. If he saw the escape pack, he did not bother to retrieve it. The pack floated under the bridge, never seen again.

All of a sudden, the air raid sirens sounded and in the distance Marvin saw two large school houses with children frantically running towards them for shelter. After walking a distance, the two men reached a small town where the guard took Marvin to a building and escorted him upstairs and shouted, "Wait!" Shortly after, a woman arrived who spoke impeccable English. She walked in and said that she lived in Kansas City for twenty years. Marvin found it funny that she spoke so sincerely and sympathetically about Kansas, his parents, sisters and brothers and she then started crying to an extent that she could not speak any longer. She became very emotional thinking about what his parents must be feeling, having Marvin so far away and not a thing they could do about it. The authorities in occupied Austria brought in this woman due to her English language capability, presumably to soften Marvin up and hopefully gain knowledge about Allied plans. Marvin had taken German in high school and college, but was warned under no condition should he speak the language to anybody. He should listen only to what others said and maybe learn something, but never let it be known that he could speak some German.

Soon after, two German soldiers arrived in a jeep-like vehicle and picked Marvin up and took him to an army camp. They escorted him to a large building and into a room with three desks with a secretary sitting behind each one of them. Marvin stood at the front of the room and the three desks. One of the soldiers demanded that Marvin take all of his clothes off. Marvin asked, "All of them?" The soldier answered, "All of them." Marvin disrobed and the soldier stated, "You don't have a compass." Marvin countered, "If I did you would have it…. you have my clothes!" To that the soldier demanded that Marvin bend over and stoop down. He wanted to check one more time and did not find a compass that he thought Marvin may have hidden between his buttocks. The soldier allowed Marvin to put his clothes back on and then escorted him to what Marvin thought was the orderly building where he found six or seven officers waiting for him. Marvin waited in a room with a door to the outside while the officers met in an interior room for over twenty minutes. Finally they realized that Marvin could have escaped in that time period. They then found it wise to make Marvin wait in the interior room while they met in the room with an outside entrance.

That night they took him to another camp, its location unclear to Marvin. The camp was dark with no lights on at all. The guard opened a door to what looked like a barracks building and said, "Go find a bunk in there." Marvin walked in and saw bunks that appeared two wide and three high. "Every time I felt a bunk there was somebody in it!" Finally, a prisoner said there was an empty bunk next to his so Marvin walked over and claimed that one. The man said, "Whatever you do, don't talk!" Marvin did not know the identity of the inmates or where they came from but they were definitely Americans. When asked the question, "You must have been really scared, even petrified." Marvin leaned back and answered,"There is no word for it...how would you have been?" I countered, "Terrified." He answered back, "That's what it was."

The next morning, the guards ordered the inmates to board a passenger train. Marvin looked up and observed that the female passengers were dressed very nicely and wore silk stockings, which he heard were not available in Germany. He remembered that silk stockings were rationed in the United

States since the material was required to manufacture parachutes. They traveled from morning until late in the day when they arrived in Frankfurt, Germany where Marvin observed the result of his squadron's previous efforts! All over the rail yard he saw engines and rail cars overturned and destroyed. The guards took Marvin to the train depot which he remembered seeing hundreds of windows in it…all bombed out!

They took Marvin along with six or seven other prisoners to a room in the basement of the train depot in Frankfurt. After about an hour, the guards escorted the men onto the street where locals lined up spitting and shouting vulgarities at them. They continued walking to a truck that eventually took the men to a place called *Dulag Luft,* near Frankfurt. *Dulag Luft* is short for the German terms *Durchgangslager der Luftwaffe*, or Transit Camp for the Air Force. Most prisoners of war were told upon arrival, "Vas Du Das Krieg Est Uber," meaning for you the war is over. *Dulag Luft* consisted of three main parts, the interrogation center at Oberursel, the Hospital at Hohemark, and the Transit Camp at Wretzlar. The camp gained a minimum of one thousand Allied flyers per month in late 1943 and increased to two thousand per month in early 1944. The peak intake of Allied prisoners of war occurred in July, 1944, with over three thousand incarcerated that month. Marvin Russell's B-17 was shot down on April 24, 1944, "smack dab in the middle".

The interrogation center possessed four barracks, two of which housed two hundred bunks that measured eight feet high, five feet wide, and twelve feet long. The administration offices were housed in the third building and the fourth contained rooms used for interrogation and for housing inmates' files and records. Like most camps, *Dulag Luft* contained a barbed wire fence exterior but prisoners were not subjected to the guard towers or flood lights commonplace to such camps. 19

Immediately upon arriving at approximately five or six o'clock in the evening, the guards took all of Marvin's clothing including pants, shirts, shoes, and socks and threw them in a pile. They issued him different clothing and took him into a cell with dimensions of ten feet in one direction and six feet in the other direction. As soon as he entered, Marvin noticed an uncovered window through which he could see outside. Soon thereafter, the guards closed the shutter to prevent escape. Marvin waited in the cell until the guards appeared handing him a lukewarm bottle of water and a slice of black bread. "I tried it and thought, I can't eat this stuff! I sat down on two by ten wood boards laid by the wall and I took that bread and I threw it under like that (he motioned throwing the bread under the two by ten foot makeshift bench). I said, "They can have it!" Marvin, knowing he could not end up dehydrated, drank most of the water and later lay upon the wooden two by ten planks and had a horrible time falling asleep. In the middle of the night, Marvin woke up hungry. He asked himself, "What to do?" He thought, "I can crawl under that two by ten bed and find that bread. It's amazing what hunger will do!" Marvin crawled underneath and found it and ate all of it.

Marvin awoke abruptly the next morning to guards whisking him away to another building. There he saw a bunch of people, mostly captured Americans. He walked in and was instantly surprised and relieved to see his two waist gunners in that very room! Marvin was directed to sit on one side of a desk and on the other side sat a German Major. Marvin said, "This we heard a lot about in the states before, they are going to give you a piece of paper to fill out." But, he was warned, "You only fill out your name, rank, and serial number." The major turned around and slid a piece of paper and a felt tip pen toward him and said in a thick German accent, "Fill it out…everything!" So Marvin filled out his name, rank, and serial number and drew a line through the remaining blanks. After filling in all the information, Marvin slid the piece of paper back to the Major to which he asked, "Is that everything?" He questioned, "Why didn't you fill out everything?" Marvin replied, "I filled out everything you're supposed to have." The Major then said, "You don't know what I'm supposed to have." So the officer gave Marvin another sheet of paper and said, "Now I want you to fill this one out completely!" Marvin filled out this form the same way he filled out the first one with his name, rank, and serial number, and lines through the blanks, as directed by American authorities. The officer had a smooth pair of leather gloves that he kept pulling through his hands over and over again while glaring at Marvin. He pushed the sheet of paper with his name, rank, and serial number filled in back to the officer. Just as soon as he took his hands off of that paper, the officer smacked Marvin's face as hard as he could with those leather gloves. Marvin acted properly as required by the Geneva Convention which states:

PART II

CAPTURE

Art. 5. Every prisoner of war is required to declare, if he is interrogated on the subject, his true names and rank, or his regimental number. If he infringes this rule, he exposes himself to a restriction of the privileges accorded to prisoners of his category. No pressure shall be exercised on prisoners to obtain information regarding the situation in their armed forces or their country. Prisoners who refuse to reply may not be

threatened, insulted, or exposed to unpleasant-
ness or disadvantages of any kind whatsoever.
If, by reason of his physical or mental condition,
a prisoner is incapable of stating his identity,
he shall be handed over to the Medical Service.
20

The officer did not abide by the rules of the Geneva
Convention. He told Marvin, "You don't understand and you'll
go back to solitary confinement until you fill the form out
completely." And in his thick German accent he continued, "We
have a man over there, next door to your cell that has been in
confinement for forty-six days. I don't think you want to stay
that long." The guard took Marvin back to the cell and worry
crowded his mind. "I went over there and I don't know why but
that afternoon they took me out of solitary confinement." Was
the guard telling Marvin the truth? Probably not since, "They
weren't telling us the truth any more than we were telling them
the truth." Most likely telling Marvin that other prisoners of war
were confined for forty-six days was a threat to encourage him to
talk. The events that followed provided a tremendous shock for
Marvin. A guard escorted him to another interrogation room in
the same building where he met another German officer who
said, "We've looked up some information, we're not sure on all
of it but we've got to have it completed. You could have

completed it with Major so and so but you failed to do so." The interrogator started reading from a book which included personal information as to where Marvin grew up, where he went to high school, where he attended college, how many brothers and sisters he had and their ages. He knew that Marvin formerly worked at the Emerson Electric Company in St. Louis following his one year stint in college. How did they learn this information? They obtained the information the same way the Americans gathered intelligence about the Germans. Marvin was told that they read every newspaper ever published in the United States. A department within the government had the responsibility of sifting through all the newspapers to find out as much as they could on certain people. Once they learned where Marvin grew up, they read every newspaper from the surrounding area. To this day, Marvin wonders how they learned so much from reading the newspapers because he does not think the newspaper companies published information regarding his brothers and sisters. "I don't know how they did it, but they even knew their names!"

Nine
Stalag 17 B

In late April or the first of May, 1944, the Germans escorted Marvin and his fellow prisoners, to the train depot where they boarded a forty and eight. The rail car, referred to as a forty and eight, carried either forty men or eight mules. Luckily Marvin said, "I was with the forty and not the eight! Straw lay all across the floor of the rail car, allowing the men some semblance of comfort. They spent four days traveling to their new destination, prisoner of war camp, Stalag 17 B in Krems, Austria. Every morning the train stopped out in the country to allow everyone to disembark the train and relieve themselves. Upon arriving at the camp, guards took them to a building on a hill that overlooked the camp for processing. They shaved their heads and it looked like they might get a chance to shower, which happened rarely. The guards corralled them down the hill to the prison camp where they assigned each prisoner to a barracks. "Gosh, anyone I had ever seen in the army before was down there! I'll tell you, it was like going home!" Six men from Marvin's crew were prisoners in the same camp and four were assigned to a different camp. After interrogation and solitary confinement, seeing some of his comrades was a welcome sight.

Following the annexation of Austria in 1938, the

21. Daily life at Stalag XVII B

22. Guard tower at Stalag XVII B

Germans used confiscated land from nearby farms in order to construct a civilian dulag and concentration camp near Krems Austria. After war commenced, following the invasion of Poland, the camp was used to house Polish prisoners of war. These same prisoners were used to construct the camp that became Stalag 17 B. The camp initially contained tents used to house prisoners, but grew rapidly to include concrete barracks that housed officers and forty wooden barracks to house enlisted prisoners. The population grew to an extent of forty thousand inmates within the camp confines, far more than the camp was designed to house, forcing inmates to sleep in barracks, washrooms and on the floor itself. Another sixty thousand worked in nearby farms and armament factories. Polish prisoners were the first occupants followed by Belgian and French soldiers following the fall of those countries in 1940. The rules below depict the guidelines prisoners followed. 23

GEF. MANNSCHAFTSSTAMMLAGER XVII B
GNEIXENDORF
TEILLAGER DER LUFTWAFFE
LAGERFÜHRUNG

JAN. 1, 1944

CAMP REGULATIONS

EVERY GERMAN OFFICER MUST BE SALUTED. WHEN SALUTING, HANDS OUT OF POCKETS, CIGARETTES AND PIPES OUT OF M
ALL GERMAN SOLDIERS IN CHARGE OF ADMINISTRATIVE OR GUARD FUNCTIONS (INCLUDING AUXILARY GUARDS EITHER IN UN
R IN CIVIL CLOTHES WITH ARMBANDS) AND ALL ARMED FORCE OFFICIALS, IF ON DUTY, ARE SUPERIORS TO THE PRIS
 WAR. THEIR ORDERS HAVE TO BE EXECUTED UNCONDITIONALLY AND IMMEDIATELY.
ROLL CALL IS MILITARY DUTY! SO BLOUSE AND OVERCOAT BUTTONED, MILITARY (NOT CIVIL) CAP AND SHOES!
EVERYONE WHO AT SIGNAL FOR ROLL CALL, DOES NOT FALL OUT IMMEDIATELY AND DIRECTLY SHOWS DISREGARD
ARDS HIS COMRADES ALREADY STANDING ROLL CALL.
ONLY THOSE HAVING A SPECIAL WRITTEN PERMIT FOR A SPECIFIED TIME FROM THE DOCTOR ARE ALLOWED IN THE BARRACKS DURING ROLL
WHILE ON PARADE KEEP QUIET, AND OBSERVE MILITARY DISCIPLINE (NO SHOUTING, SMOKING, NOR PLAYING)!
AFTER ROLL CALL LEAVE IN FULL ORDER (NO RUNNING FROM PARADE GROUND)!
ALL PRISONERS OF WAR, EXCEPT UNABLE, HAVE TO CARRY OUT WORKS CONCERNING THEIR OWN BENEFIT. THOSE REFUSING TO WORK WILL BE FO
CHOW DETAIL, WHEN WHISTLED OUT, HAVE TO FALL OUT IMMEDIATELY
EVERYBODY TO BE DELIVERED INTO INFIRMARY, ISOLATION OR HOSPITAL, AS WELL AS SUCH DETATCHED TO SPECIAL W
R SERVICES, HAVE TO GIVE THEIR NAMES, SECOND NAMES AND NUMBERS TO THEIR BARRACK CHIEF WHO HAS TO INFORM THE RESPECTIVE GERMAN CC
IF.
PRISONERS OF WAR IN ISOLATION ARE NOT ALLOWED TO PAY VISITS OUTSIDE OF ISOLATION NOR TO RECEIVE VISITORS NOT
THOSE TOUCHING WARNING WIRE OR ENTERING AREA WARNED NOT TO WILL BE FIRED ON WITHOUT WARNING
HANGING UP LAUNDRY, BLANKETS ETC. ON ANY BARBED WIRE IS STRICTLY PROHIBITED. HANG THEM ON THE STAKES DESTINED FOR THIS PU
MISPLACING DOG-TAGS HAS TO BE REPORTED AT ONCE.
PRISONERS OF WAR WHO HAVE TO LEAVE CAMP FOR ANY REASON (E.G. FOR HOSPITAL, DELOUSING, WORKS OUTSIDE OF CAMP
UNLOADING RED CROSS PARCELS) ARE NOT ALLOWED MORE THAN ONE PACKAGE OF CIGARETTES OR TOBACCO. EXCESSIVE QU
LL BE CONFISCATED.
ADDRESS REQUIREMENTS, WISHES ETC. ONLY TO YOUR BARRACK CHIEF WHO WILL PASS THEM ON TO THE GERMAN COMP
IEF.
CONSULTING HOURS FOR GERMAN "COMPANY CHIEFS" ONLY FROM 9 - 10 AND 15 - 16 O'CLOCK BY BARRACK CHIEFS O

(GEZ.) KÜHN
OBERST u. KOMMAND

KREMS/GNEIXENDORF

24. Aerial photograph of Stalag XVII B

You can see Marvin's barracks number 30 B located to the right of the two circles at the top of the picture. It is the second barracks to the right.

Russian prisoners began arriving at the camp following the start of Operation Barbarossa in the summer of 1941, commencing the eastern front of the war following the failure of Hitler's plan to force Britain to surrender during the Battle of Britain. American flyers were being captured at such staggering rates which forced the Germans to relocate thousands of Russian prisoners to camps throughout Austria. Stalag 17 B was the largest prisoner of war camp in Austria and the third largest in Nazi occupied Europe. 25

The Germans mostly followed the Geneva Convention protocol relating to forced labor. Officers could not be forced to work and sergeants could only take supervisory roles.

SECTION III
WORK OF PRISONERS OF WAR

CHAPTER 1

General

> Art. 27. Belligerents may employ as work-
> men prisoners of war who are physically fit,
> other than officers and persons of equivalent
> statue, according to their rank and their ability.
> Nevertheless, if officers or persons of equivalent
> status ask for suitable work, this shall be found
> for them as far as possible. Noncommissioned
> officers who are prisoners of war may be
> compelled to undertake only supervisory

work, unless they expressly request remuner-
ative occupation. 26

Marvin, a sergeant, was a non-commissioned officer and
thus relieved of having to complete hard labor or menial tasks
that his counterparts in the Pacific endured in Japanese prisoner
of war camps. In the United States, the policy differed and
sergeants or non-commissioned officers were required to work in
prisoner of war camps.

Approximately 5,200 Sergeants in addition to three
officers (a chaplain and the two doctors) lived in the prison
camp. The Germans used electricity sparingly, turning on the
lights only when they had a need which forced the P.O.W.s to
limit any activities to daylight hours. There was no heat in the
barracks with snow and ice all around and temperatures
averaging close to zero degrees. The prisoners had no hot water,
but did have access to water that was about thirty-eight degrees
in the washroom. There were no laundry facilities of any kind.
They wore the same clothes day and night and were deloused
approximately every six months.

The prisoners elected an overall president and vice-
president of the camp. Each barracks had a German chief as
well as an American chief. Marvin recalled an event that
occurred seven years earlier where the name of his German

barracks chief was mentioned. In 1937, Marvin, his father, uncle and brother, Delton, traveled to Kansas City where Marvin's father purchased a Co-Op tractor with the capability of traveling sixty-five miles per hour. Delton drove the tractor home while his father, his uncle, and he rode together. In the town of Cottonwood Falls, they decided to stop to eat. They looked out the window as Delton drove the tractor past the restaurant and did not give it a second thought until they were under way after eating. "When we finished eating, we went four to five miles and we saw the tractor but no one on it." Delton ran out of gasoline and walked to the nearest farmhouse for help. The farmer remarked that as soon as the fight was over they were listening to on the radio was over they would help him. The fight that night was between Joe Lewis and Max Schmeling. Marvin commented, "Of course, Joe Lewis won." Who knew that Max Schmeling would be Marvin's German barracks chief at Stalag 17 B seven years later! An inmate named Ned Handy experienced a run in with a guard named Max in which he described:

> After dressing, I was the last out, trailing the others, when suddenly I was grabbed by my left arm and yanked about ten feet to a little shed. I was thrown through its rickety door before I could even react. My attacker was

strong and he spun me around. It was Max....
He drew a large pistol from his holster,
moved the barrel to his right hand and swung
its heavy butt hard into my head. He hit me
two or three more times before I blacked out. 27

Marvin remembers hearing the word, "Raus!" or get out
over and over as the guards always yelled commands to the
prisoners. Chain of command was very important in camp
organization and directives were passed down from Nazi camp
leaders to the president and vice-president of the prisoners of war
to the chief of each barracks.

Every morning and every night, usually at twelve

28. Formation at Stalag XVII B

o'clock, the prisoners stood in formation, four deep. Standing in formation meant standing quietly and being counted by the guards. In order to be dismissed from formation, the Compound Chief, Major Eigle, would raise his right hand in salute, and would yell, "HEIL".

Approximately every three to four weeks, the prisoners would be called out of the barracks and marched in front of a table that was set up for the occasion. Two German officers were seated behind the table. As the prisoners marched by, their dog tags were checked to be sure they matched the one in the records.

The prisoner of war camp relied on water that came from the Alps. It was cold! The water entered the barracks at thirty-eight degrees Fahrenheit. The prisoners were allowed only two showers in the thirteen months Marvin was a prisoner of war at Stalag 17 B. Once every six months the men were ushered to a bath house up on a hill in the camp. "There were 5,200 of us in the camp, all Americans, all sergeants, and all flyers and they would take us in there a barracks at a time." The Germans yelled, "Take off all your clothes!" Then the guards took all the inmates' lice infested clothes to get de- loused. There were fifteen water spigots in the shower house and two men were ordered to share one spigot. The Germans

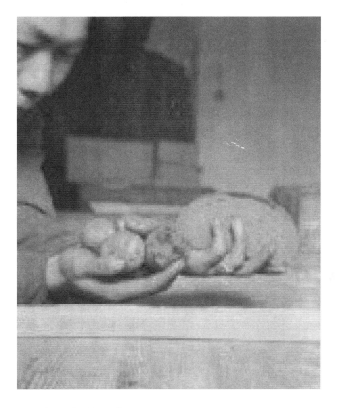

29. One day's rations

turned the warm water on for about five minutes then turned on the cold water for about a minute, ending the shower. After the shower, everyone got a closely clipped haircut, just like a shaved head. That was their chance at cleanliness until the next opportunity came six months later.

Breakfast consisted of a cup of hot water and for lunch the men were given a cup of barley or rye soup. For other meals, the men ate whatever was in season. If carrots were in season, the men received two of them and for at least six weeks when rutabagas were in season the prisoners received only one (and it was unpeeled and uncooked) a day and nothing else! "People don't know why I don't like rutabagas but I don't particularly care for rutabagas!" When available, the Germans provided boiled potatoes, although a rarity. Marvin recounted, "I never saw a potato bigger than a golf ball." Much of the food the men received was grown locally, dug up out of the ground and given to the men who waited in long lines. Once a prisoner made his way to the front of the line, a prisoner dipped a ladle in a large kettle and dumped the contents into a small bowl that each man was issued.

The Red Cross sent shoebox-size containers of food to P.O.W. camps throughout Nazi occupied Europe. Their contents mainly included canned tuna fish, cheese, powdered milk, margarine, sugar, cigarettes, and chocolate. Although the Red Cross provided enough food in these boxes to feed each prisoner for a week, most of the rations never made it to the intended recipients. German soldiers confiscated the supplies en route to the prison camps. In most cases, prisoners only received one or two boxes of rations during their entire imprisonment let alone seven per week. 30

Since food was so scarce, men took extreme measures in an attempt to satisfy their hunger. A cat lived in the prison with three kittens. One had a crippled foot and walked on its front knee instead of its paw. All of the prisoners played with the cats, as they were a distraction from the daily grind of camp. One day the men received word that other prisoners were killing the cats and eating them. Marvin said, "Maybe there's one left." It just so happened that no one took the crippled kitten. A fellow inmate named Andrew, said, "I will go look for it!" Marvin and Andrew butchered it and took kindling from the barracks and any paper they could find to start a fire. "I don't know if water even got to the boiling point, but we kept sampling it trying to see if it was cooked enough over two or three days, but we ate it anyway and it was gone. Once the cooking began, quite a crowd massed and everyone wanted a taste. That is hunger at its worst."

Marvin encountered another "treat" around Christmastime, 1944. Beforehand, a typical breakfast consisted of a cup of hot water but on this particular Christmas, he and the other men received a cup of oatmeal including a bowl and a tin spoon. He slept on the top of a pair of bunks where he took his oatmeal and looked forward to savoring it. All of a sudden a long worm with a black head floated to the top of his oatmeal.

"It must have been over an inch long, as long as my index finger." Marvin climbed down from his bunk and proclaimed to everyone, "Look at what I've got!" It was quite the find for a starving prisoner of war. The rest of the men said, "Give him to me. I want him! Let me eat him!" Marvin recalled, "I took it and ate it. It was good because I had that much to eat. I was so hungry it didn't make any difference what I ate. It didn't matter what I put in my mouth, by that point it tasted like the oatmeal!" Three weeks after liberation Marvin weighed in at one hundred and nine pounds. Keep in mind that in those three weeks he had access to more and better quality food. There is no way to tell what Marvin weighed while at Stalag 17 B but his best guess was that it was around ninety pounds.

Toward the end of May, 1944 Marvin and some of the others realized that Memorial Day was approaching. They decided to recognize the day by attending a service at the chapel the guards converted out of one of the barracks. That morning prisoners packed inside and outside the makeshift chapel. "Everybody was going to come no matter what denomination," Marvin remembered. They came to honor the country they fought for and hoped one day soon would be liberated. The men bellowed out the words to 'God Bless America' as loud as possible. "I would say that if anyone was standing outside in

America, they could have heard us!" Fortunately, the singing did not bother the Germans too much.

Marvin remembered three American officers interned in the camp. Two were medics and one a Chaplin, all captains. The Germans integrated the men with the rest of the prisoners as "I don't think they knew about segregation." Prisoners in Stalag 17 B were "separated by nothing. If you were a prisoner, that's what you were." Ethnicity was the exception to this policy of no separation among prisoners. Russian prisoners were housed in a different section of Stalag 17 B where they fared much worse than their American counterparts with a death rate of five to six per day. "They would walk by us carrying the dead ones to a cemetery, their leg was the same size from the hip all the way down to the ankle." The Soviet Union was not a partner to the 1929 Geneva Convention which meant they were not protected against inhumane treatment.

> Detested, feared, and treated worse than animals by the Germans, Russian prisoners suffered beyond comprehension. The Nazis ignored sickness and starvation in the Russian's ranks, and men died in droves. Desperately hungry during the winter months, Russian prisoners propped up dead comrades in their lines for roll calls each morning to be counted by unknowing Germans, who issued rations based on a shoe count. 31

In contrast, German prisoners of war in camps in the United States often had more rights than black Americans, most notably in the south. One such camp, located in central Georgia allowed its internees to attend movies in town. The prisoners could sit in the lower level with other white patrons while black patrons were forced to sit in the balcony, away from the others.

The 5,200 American prisoners were housed in barracks that contained roughly three hundred men each. The barracks measured thirty feet by two hundred and forty feet. Each barrack contained a washroom, and triple high bunks, but no stove. Between two and three hundred prisoners all shared one latrine during nighttime hours and dysentery and diarrhea spread uncontrollably. 32 The bunks contained plywood surfaces and each man had a very thin mattress, partially filled with excelsior (wood shavings). "Once in a while on a sunny day, the Germans allowed the prisoners to hang their mattress sacks out in the sun to get the lice out." Marvin added that American prisoner of war camps contained barracks of similar size that housed only thirty-five inmates.

On Thanksgiving Day, 1944, Marvin awoke to desperate cries from a prisoner in a bunk across the barracks. Evidently he became very sick. The men sought permission from the Germans for the two American medics to help him. The doctors

33. Prisoner of war cleaning out his bed mattress

34. Sketch of the inside of a barracks building at Stalag XVII B

both agreed that the man had a very bad case of appendicitis and that he must be operated on immediately or he would die. A hospital sat on a nearby hill inside the confines of the camp. The Germans went to the hospital and came back and said, "He can't have surgery here, the doctors are all drunk!" The American doctors explained that they could perform surgery but had no anesthesia or anything to dull the pain. The only thing they could do was cut him open, take his appendix out and sew him back up. Instead of a regular knife they only had a razor with which to operate. At around five o'clock that night after the surgery, they brought him back to the barracks. Later Marvin learned that the man had to be held down by other prisoners due to the intense pain.

Prison camp stories differed depending on who told the them. Every man had his own version of what occurred, depending on their individual circumstances. The Germans attempted to prevent any prisoners from escaping by constructing dual barbed wire fences with towers manned by Germans with machine guns. However, that did not prevent some internees from attempting to flee the confines of Stalag 17 B. Marvin heard about prisoners that planned to escape and how they collected as much food as possible from Red Cross supplies. Even though most prisoners were loyal to the cause of escaping their German guards, obviously some were not, as various prisoners told the Germans about the plan to escape.

Another attempt involved prisoners who attempted to dig a tunnel under the steps of barrack 40, using tin cans as shovels to get them under the warning wire to the outside fences and watchful eye of the Nazi guards equipped with machine guns. 35 The attempted escape was a failure. Those hoping to escape planned on crawling through the tunnel during the night. Apparently the Germans discovered the plan. A few minutes before the planned escape, lights came on all over the prison camp. German guards entered barracks 40 A and quickly put a stop to the planned escape. Marvin does not know what types of punishment the Germans inflicted on the perpetrators, or even if the Germans knew which of the prisoners attempted escape. To thwart further prisoner attempts at escape, the Germans demolished barracks 40 A, located near the camp fence to prevent inmates from digging tunnels from the barracks to outside the camp. Prior to demolition, one of these barracks housed a chapel. 36

Black markets existed in most P.O.W. camps which allowed prisoners to obtain parts to make radios. This enabled them to learn from the radio updates on Allied advances from the British Broadcasting Stations or the American Armed Forces

37. Prisoners sorting through Red Cross parcels

network.

A French P.O.W. camp existed adjacent to Stalag 17 B. They traded radio parts with the Americans in exchange for cigarettes. Before departing for the front, most G.I.'s received rations of cigarettes and the best brands as well, either Chesterfield or Lucky Strikes. The fact that the French were on better terms with the Germans than the Americans, allowed them to trade or barter. Every day the men received updates from one of the barracks inmates who would listen to the radio with a headset. This was highly forbidden by the Germans, so one inmate stood watch at each of the barracks' entrances to watch for approaching guards.

Marvin awoke one morning to an unexpected happening. It was stipulated in the Geneva Convention that any P.O.W. that was wounded beyond combat capabilities would be exchanged for a similar enemy P.O.W. The Germans agreed to repatriation, meaning they agreed to prisoner exchanges with the enemy. The Germans agreed to exchange prisoners who were disabled, for example with one leg, and who could no longer fight. This ensured the prisoner would no longer fight and be a threat to the Germans. The Geneva Convention agreed upon plan called for one American exchanged for one German. When the time came, the Germans agreed to exchange one American for every five German prisoners given back to them. One of Marvin's fellow inmates was included in the prisoner exchange. Without a whole lot to do, time passed extremely slowly. Though Marvin could not visualize exactly how he would get out, he dreamed of the day he would get the opportunity to leave the confines of the prison camp.

By way of radio broadcasts made from the prisoners' black market contacts, Marvin and the others learned about advancing American and Allied troops. They heard about Operation Overlord, or D-Day, the largest amphibious invasion in history, hoping that the invasion of France meant hastening the war's end. Marvin remembers worrying that the invasion would not be a success due to the heavily defended Atlantic Wall on the English Channel. Though problems existed, D-Day proved a success and within six months the liberation of France occurred and the Allies readied themselves to invade Germany.

Ten
The Beginning of the End

Following Stalingrad, commonly agreed to as the turning point in the German war in the east, the Russians spent the next two years repelling the Germans west and pushing them closer and closer to Stalag 17 B. As the Russians advanced, the prisoners began to sense uneasiness among the German guards. They feared capture by the Russians, preferring to face the Americans, advancing from the west.

One morning, the Germans ordered the prisoners to move towards the American lines. The prisoners had a sit-down strike. The Germans said, "You are hurting yourselves. We are trying to help you." According to Marvin, "The Russians were really

38. Map of Europe and P.O.W. camps

not our friends." On April 8, 1945, over four thousand men began an almost three hundred mile forced march from Krems, Austria. Over a month later, on May 9, the Russians liberated the nine hundred prisoners that remained in the camp as they were too ill to march. 39

Many men did not have adequate shoes, resulting in blistering, cracking, and bleeding feet. The Germans divided the massive group of prisoners into eight groups consisting of five hundred men in each led by one American and twenty German Volkssturm or Nazi Party militia members. 40 Food was scarce, forcing the men to eat whatever they could find, including worms, bugs, weeds, and grass.

They marched at least twenty kilometers per day for six weeks. In the midst of this hellish march, Marvin could not help but notice and appreciate the beautiful countryside. At night, the men slept in dug out holes in manure piles to keep warm. The Russians took over Stalag 17 B a few days after the prisoners evacuated.

As the prisoners set out marching along the Linz River, the Germans carried materials in three or four horse drawn wagons. One day it rained extremely hard and one of the dehydrated and exhausted horses slipped and fell underneath the wagon resulting in a broken leg. Without any way to ease its suffering, the guards decided to kill the horse. The men did get some good soup from the horse meat. Once in a while the marching men passed a farm that had a grainery allowing them to eat rye or barley. They marched until they came to the Danube River and Marvin describes it as beautiful blue with rock walls. Marvin remembers seeing large green lawns that came up to the Danube with the bluest water, kept up perfectly even during the war. What a contrast to the bleakness he and the thousands of others endured in the prisoner of war camps and now on this forced march away from the Russians.

Still walking along the Danube River and after days without eating hardly anything, the men walked on a green expanse of lawn that contained hundreds, if not thousands of snails 'that big' (and Marvin used his thumb and index finger to model how big they measured.) One of the other prisoners commented that if you put the snail on your tongue you could suck him out of his shell. Sure enough you could! "I had a little bag made out of a towel and I put as many as I could in that towel so I would have something to eat later. They were good eating but I would say it took thirty minutes to chew one up. It didn't taste too bad but they weren't cooked and hard to chew." Later on, in the march heading west from Krems, the guards ordered the men to stop for the night. Marvin, and two of his friends, named Hubert Matlock and Levi Burns, walked up to a barn and found a tub of lard, hidden in a hay loft, apparently saved for future cooking. Shortly afterwards, others heard about their find and soon the place was swarming with prisoners stuffing their faces with that lard. The farm complex contained a cow lot, surrounded by a house, the barn, a machine shed, and a chicken house. In the cow lot, the men saw an old hen with eight to ten chickens. Marvin laughed as he commented on how stupid the men were in choosing the old hen over the younger chickens which had more and better quality meat. By this time, the chickens shrieked constantly, alerting the Gestapo. One of them approached a prisoner and asked if he took the chicken. The man replied that, "We had to have it, we are starving." In return, he hit him across the face with his rifle and broke his nose. To that Marvin responded, "That chicken probably wasn't worth it!"

The six week march to Braunau, Austria Hitler's birth place at the bottom of the Alps proved very traumatic and something that Marvin remembers well into his 90s. There were hundreds, if not thousands of Jews on one of Hitler's notorious death marches. They were nothing but skin and bone and when they were so weak that they fell to the ground, the Germans jabbed them with their bayonets and killed them. The American P.O.W.s marched down a long hill on the right hand side of the road and the Jews marched up the hill on the left hand side. After the last formation of the Jews, a long bed truck followed up the hill with two or three men walking alongside and picking up the bodies and tossing them on the truck, one man picking up the body by the arms and the other by the feet. There was so much blood it ran like a stream down the path which Marvin marched. There was a bridge over a creek that they had to cross, and the blood from the slain Jews ran off to the right into the creek. The water on the other side of the bridge was clear until it mixed with the blood. They marched about three quarters of a mile past the bridge and in an area to the right, Marvin and his fellow P.O.W.s witnessed thousands of Jews lined up in some sort of formation, marching to their demise.

When they reached Hitler's birth place, the American P.O.W.s were taken to a warehouse when the guards eventually decided to leave to find lunch. The prisoners saw twenty-five to thirty rifles leaning up against one of the walls. The other prisoners began taking the bayonets off the rifles, "So, I took one too! I took the cover off the bayonet and saw blood on one side of the blade." It is surprising that the Germans allowed prisoners to take possession of weapons that potentially might threaten their control. Marvin countered, "They didn't care. As far as they were concerned the war was over."

They marched until they came to a clearing of trees with brush in the middle with guard houses built on the four corners. Not knowing what the future held, Marvin guessed that was where they were going to stay until the war was over. Marvin, along with the two waist gunners built a teepee made of sticks and brush in which to sleep. The teepee was only big enough to sleep the three of them. Two to three inches of snow fell during the night. About a fortnight later, Marvin's attention was drawn across the river. "We were on the south side of the Linz River, and on the north side we saw white flags go up and tanks pass through. My heart skipped a beat: They were American tanks…! It meant to us that the war was nearly over."

Up ahead a welcome sight approached an American Sherman tank. The captain on the tank said he did not know whether or not to stop, but he did. Before he knew it, over five thousand of the prisoners crowded around the tank. It so happened that they were trying to keep up with the marching prisoners as well as Patton's Third Army and got ahead of the 13th Armored Division. The 13th had planned on liberating the P.O.W.s while the 15th Armored Division did not know about them. Seeing the prisoners was a surprise to the captain who was attached to the 15th. The P.O.W. officers and the Captain of the 15th Armored Division talked for a while and the Captain said, "Well, I'll go down there, but I can't do anything for your men yet." Even if he possessed the capability to assist, the swarming men made it impossible for the tank to leave. He stood atop of the tank and said, "I am glad to be here but I am sorry I can't do more to help you." He promised that as soon as he could, "I will get word back and I will get a truck load of bread out here, one loaf for each one of you." The army came in and took all the German guards, which was a definite relief to the prisoners. Marvin's reaction, "It was great! We were going to get to go home!" The bread arrived the next day. One loaf per person as the captain promised. It was a daunting process logistically to provide transportation home for thousands of prisoners but there finally was light at the end of the tunnel.

The Germans made a habit of blowing up bridges toward the end of the war to slow the advancing Allied armies. The Americans ordered a German officer to help build a pontoon bridge across the river. The officer replied that he did not have to work due to his rank. The Americans put a bullet through his head. Near the camp sat an airfield across the pontoon bridge and soon, American planes began to land. The next day C-47's hauling in five gallon cans of gasoline arrived. "They would haul in gasoline and take us out."

Marvin and his fellow airmen arrived in Reims, France on the eighth day of May, around seven o'clock. General Eisenhower was in Reims, scheduled to sign the Peace Treaty at eight o'clock, officially ending the European War. "I was there," commented Marvin. A short time later they took a bus to Camp Lucky Strike. Following the German surrender in May, 1945, most American soldiers fighting in the European Theater of Operations worried that they would be sent to the Pacific for the eventual invasion of Japan. Rumors spread about the jungle fighting, malaria, and of course the atrocities committed in prisoner of war camps in Japan. Marvin and the rest of the over five thousand prisoners of war from Stalag 17 B, in addition to the thousands of others recently liberated from camps all across Europe, did not have that fear since former P.O.W.s had the chance of going straight home, with an end to their military service. There was a point system for all military servicemen and women to be eligible for discharge, but for the liberated prisoners, they had the option of getting out of the service.

After waiting two or three weeks at Camp Lucky Strike, Marvin boarded a troop ship for what he calls, "a slow boat to China." With thousands of men on the ship the conditions were less than perfect but Marvin could not believe he was on his way home. After a week at sea, the ship's passengers caught sight of Miss Lady Liberty in New York Harbor miles from shore. "It was a sight to see!" The ships' decks were packed with homesick soldiers ready to move past the nightmares of war and prisoner of war camps. "I walked out ten steps and kissed the ground."

Eleven
And He Thought the Worst
Was Over...

From New York, the men went to Fort Dix, New Jersey.
There, the ex P.O.W.s were to be demobilized and while there,
allowed to make one telephone call at no charge. With
thousands of homesick men waiting to make the connection with
mothers, fathers, wives, and girlfriends, it took some time for
Marvin to reach the head of the line. When Marvin's turn came,
he hesitated nervously. While in prison camp he received ten or
eleven letters and cards from his mother. She never mentioned
his father in any of the correspondence. Marvin came to the
conclusion that his father died. At that time all mail, both
incoming and outgoing, was censored. Anything written that

was not acceptable to the censor would be blacked out. It never came to his mind that his mother's mention of his dad could have been blacked out by the censors. Marvin called the operator who made the connection to his family's farmhouse. His mother answered the telephone and almost fainted from shock. After recovering from her surprise, they talked for a while before she asked, "Do you want to talk to your dad?" With emotion, Marvin commented, "I didn't have the strength to do anything for a little bit. It got me. I never had such a feeling in my life."

From Fort Dix, New Jersey, Marvin traveled to Fort Leavenworth Army Base in Kansas. There he was issued clothing and went through a routine interrogation. It was necessary to travel to Kansas City in order to get a train home. Even though the train arrived at McPherson depot at dawn, his mother, father, brothers and sisters were all there to meet him.

Marvin was granted a ninety day terminal leave, his final furlough from his time in the service. After a short time, Marvin contracted hepatitis and was transferred to a hospital at Smoky Hill Army Air Base, in Salina, Kansas. He recovered over the course of the next six weeks which resulted in delaying Marvin's discharge from the military. After a six week sick leave and the ninety day terminal leave, Marvin was sent to Kelly Field, Texas. Arriving in the afternoon, he reported to the post theater at eight o'clock to get his discharge. "I got there and there was a Major handing out discharges. He called my name and I walked up, saluted and stuck my hand out. He said, "Russell do you realize that if you wait three more days you'll get a hash mark?" I said, "Major, I wouldn't stay three hours for a hash mark." He replied, "I don't blame you. I wouldn't either," and handed me my discharge and I went home."

Marvin's older brother, Delton, also served in the European Theater of Operations. He went in quite a bit after Marvin and served in the 15th Armored Division which also saw action near where Marvin served in Europe.

Marvin was discharged on the third of November, 1945, and was married on the twenty-fourth. The newlyweds moved into a house that his grandparents had lived in on a farm six miles from his parents' farm and things moved along smoothly. He bought several pieces of farm equipment, including a Model M International Farmall Tractor, six milk cows and three hundred baby chicks.

Marvin had been home for a while and one evening, on July 24, 1946, after milking their cows, Marvin and his wife Lois drove to Marvin's parents' home. His father said, "There is a leak in the gas line to the light system. It has been leaking all day long." Lois walked to the barn where Marvin's mother was finishing milking their cows. A butane gas engine powered a generator that charged the batteries which provided electricity to everything on the farm. The washhouse that contained the power system was approximately twenty feet north of the house. Marvin and his father walked down to the cellar to check the gas line to the engine. His father cautioned him to not turn on any lights because this gas had been leaking all day. Marvin made it down to the very last step and watched his father work. His father said he had fixed the leak when all of a sudden there was a massive explosion. A hole blew through the foundation of the washhouse providing an escape route. The explosion made the stairway unusable which forced Marvin and his father to crawl through the hole in the foundation. A neighbor heard the explosion and claimed that the washhouse blew at least fifty feet in the air. He came running over to see if they had enough gasoline to get to the hospital. Days later, when they tore the washhouse down, there was not a piece of lumber more than two feet long. The explosion was heard fifteen miles away.

Marvin, followed by his father, struggled to the garage to find some oil to put on the burns. Lois and Marvin's mother ran to them to see what happened. Lois started yelling hysterically to which Marvin countered, "Shut up, you're not hurt!" She asked about what looked like a handkerchief dangling on

Marvin's arm but really it was the skin from his arm hanging loosely. He grabbed the garage door handle which caused all the skin to fall off the palm of his hand. Lois opened the door for him. He attempted to use his other hand to unscrew the top of the oil can when the skin came off of it as well. Again, Lois took the top off the oil can.

Marvin's mother drove them to McPherson Hospital, and during the journey Marvin commented, "I hollered and screamed the whole way!" Apparently his father came out of shock and started screaming from pain until they arrived. His mother never drove over fifty miles per hour but on this trip she drove so fast that the speedometer was against the peg the entire way.

At the hospital, the doctors called in several others to help. They bandaged up Marvin and his father to the best of their ability but informed them that they needed more extensive treatment. Marvin's mother said Eddie Woods was going to drive Marvin to the Veterans Hospital in Wichita, and asked if he remembered him. Marvin replied, "Yes, I knew that he used to work at the Piggly Wiggly. He was alright when he wasn't drunk but he was drunk most of the time!" They had a police escort from McPherson Hospital to the Veteran's Hospital in Wichita.

Marvin's sister, LeVonne, was going through nurse's

training in Hutchison and when her employers heard of the
accident they told her to report to the Veteran's hospital while
remaining on the payroll. Within a few hours LeVonne arrived,
helping care for her father and brother.

The Army was notified that Marvin and his father were
critically injured, and Delton was needed at home. Delton was
stationed near Frankfurt, Germany but due to the circumstances
was immediately discharged and sent home. He landed in
Wichita and took a cab to the hospital. When he walked in and
saw Marvin's burned body, he immediately fainted.

Over the course of the next three weeks, doctors
informed Marvin's wife and mother that he would not survive.
Marvin's father had a better chance of living as his body was
only fifty percent burned. Doctors said that no one who had
ninety percent of their body burned, like Marvin, ever lived.
Bandages, about ten inches square and one inch thick were
placed all over the burned areas. Penicillin was discovered and
put into use in 1945. Marvin was required to have a shot every
three hours which continued throughout his entire
hospitalization. The injections had to be administered to his feet
until other parts of his body healed. I.V.s were inserted in
Marvin's head and feet, and along with routine medicines, he
was given blood plasma on a regular basis. Marvin could not

eat anything so he was fed using intravenous therapy. Right after Marvin was hospitalized, doctors advised that he drink as much water as possible but that was impossible without the use of a straw. He was required to pass three gallons of urine a day, therefore was given an abundance of water to drink.

After five or six months of healing, the doctors worked to begin applying skin grafts. Marvin was supposed to go to a hospital in Kansas City in order for Dr. Hebert to perform the skin grafts, using a machine he invented to peel off the correct number of layers of skin. While waiting for transportation to take him to Kansas City, Marvin's regular doctor, Dr. Herwich, told Marvin that Dr. Hebert had died within the last twenty minutes. Several weeks later, another specialist came to Wichita to perform the skin graft surgery. In all, Marvin endured thirteen skin grafts operations over a period of three to four months.

Marvin beat the odds and recovered fully from the burns. Considering all the misery Marvin endured during this fifteen month period, one good thing did happen. Lois gave birth to their first child. It was a boy, and they named him Eugene Wesley.

42. The newspaper clipping from July 26, 1946 on the following page is courtesy of the Canton Pilot

Alex R. Chrzanowski

Neighbors Plow For Injured Vet

Twenty-four friends of Mr and Mrs. Marvin Russell brought their tractors early Monday morning and started plowing on his 140 acre wheat field. By two o'clock in the afternoon, just as the first drops of rain began to fall, the last tractor pulled out of the field, with its task completed.

The following men brought their tractors: Aaron Koehn, Elmer Koehn, Victor Koehn, John P. Kliewer, Glen Hamilton, Milford Blair, Charles Tinsley, Preston Waln, Reynold Hintz, Joel McNees, Clifford Leffler, Floyd Sellers, G. C. Dresher, Garland Sadey, Brown Griffith, Bailey Griffith, Galen Barrett, Raymond Smith, Jonas Ratzlaff, Fred Shultz Howard Lewis on Bill Bandy's tractor, G. E. Williams on Art Colby's tractor, Delton Russell on Marvin Russell's tractor, Bryce Russel on D. L. Russell's tractor. Lester Hamilton and Clifford Blair acted as roustabouts and supplied the needs of all the men working.

Mrs. Charles Tinsley, Mrs. Lucien Russel, Mrs. Clifford Blair, Mrs. Clifford Leffler and Mrs. Glen Hamilton, Mrs. Preston A. Waln, Mrs. Raymond Smith, Mrs. Delton Russell and Mrs. D. L. Russell all came with well filled baskets and helped Mrs. Marvin Russell serve the hungry men at noon.

Marvin and his father, D. L. Russell, who were severely burned in a butane gas explosion last July 24 are still patients in the Veterans hsopital in Wichita, but hope to be home in the near future.

FATHER, SON HURT IN BLAST

McPherson, Kas., July 25. (AP)—Daniel R. Russell, 52, World War 1 veteran, and his son, Marvin, 24, a veteran of World War II, were injured critically last night when a butane plant exploded in the back yard of their farm home northwest of Canton.

They were given emergency treatment at the McPherson Hospital and then taken to the Veterans Hospital at Wichita where their condition today was described as critical.

The butane plant was located in a wash house. The father and son had been repairing a leak, and the explosion resulted when they started the motor. The building housing the plant was wrecked completely.

120

Lois and the children, Pittsburg, Kansas
Courtesy of Marvin Russell

While Marvin recovered from his wounds, he and Lois received help on the farm from his parents, brothers and friends. The doctor stated, "Get off the farm if you want to heal!" His tractor, milk cows, calves, and chickens were sold at public auction. Since he rented the farmland, luckily he did not have to worry about selling it. Shortly thereafter, they moved to Pittsburg, Kansas. Marvin obtained employment at J.C. Penney selling shoes before working at the Kansas Ordinance Plant as gauge inspector. His previous employment at Emerson Electric appealed to Captain Weiss who ended up hiring Marvin. The plant manufactured one hundred and five millimeter shells and two hundred fifty and five hundred pound bombs.

One day Marvin and Lois went to the grocery store and after shopping, Eugene followed a lady out the door who checked out at the register ahead of them. She did not know Eugene was behind her and as she walked out he was in the middle of the doorway. The door swung back and hit Eugene knocking him on his back where his head hit the marble floor. He cried hysterically whereupon Marvin called the doctor who asked if he had a bump on his head. If not, they were told not to worry about it. He seemed fine for a couple of weeks but then he suddenly came down with an illness. Lois and Marvin took Eugene to the hospital where the doctors treated him for an ear problem and discharged him.

Over the course of the next three months, Eugene seemed to improve and one night asked his father if he would swing him, which Marvin did. Lois called them to dinner when Eugene had to use the bathroom. Lois took him and before she knew it, the boy relieved himself on the bathtub. He started quivering and after, Marvin again called the doctor who directed them to get Eugene to the hospital. They gave him ether until they could stop the convulsions but suddenly he lost consciousness. They took him from Pittsburg, Kansas to the hospital in Kansas City.

Lois and Eugene at eight and a half months
Courtesy of Marvin Russell

The doctors asked Marvin and Lois if he had been hit on the head to which they said no. After a few days, the doctor asked if they could perform an autopsy on their son to which they replied, "No not yet, he's not dead!" A few days later he did indeed die and an autopsy was performed. He in fact experienced a trauma to his head from the door at the grocery store. They learned at that time that Lois was expecting their third child. Marvin did not think that they could handle a pregnancy at that time and asked the doctor if it could be terminated. The doctor said, "No I can't and I wouldn't! It's the best thing to happen to you." Lois and Marvin had two more boys and a girl. Eugene's death provided a reunion of sorts for Marvin and some of his fellow P.O.W.s. He asked four of them to serve as pall bearers at the funeral for his son providing a sad reunion for his former comrades.

In 1956, Marvin received a telephone call from Redstone Arsenal in Huntsville, Alabama. They offered to transfer Marvin from Kansas Ordinance Plant to work at Redstone Arsenal, because the Korean War was ending. Due to a housing shortage in Huntsville, he rented a shared room at a boarding house. Marvin left his wife and children at home in Pittsburg, while he figured out living arrangements. The only way to find a house was to have one built.

Redstone Arsenal consisted of two components, NASA and Missile Command. His job was to inspect missile parts. After two weeks inspecting the NIKE B missile in Kalamazoo, Michigan, there was a problem relating to welding and was later rejected. After the failure of the NIKE B, he was reassigned to work on the TSQ 73, equipment set up for border patrol security which possessed the radar capability to detect any aircraft or ship coming into United States airspace or into U.S. waters (and to detect whether they were friend or foe).

While working on these two products, the Nike B and TSQ 73, Marvin and his friend and partner, Charles Richardson were busy building thirteen houses. Since there was a housing shortage they decided to help satisfy the demand. By 1961, the need for building houses had slowed down and Marvin went into business opening a Mugs Up Root Beer drive-in watering hole. Two years later he opened a second one. During the summer months he employed approximately fifty people. One of his most memorable experiences during this time centered around occasional stops from busses loaded with Grand Ole Opry entertainers that came in for refreshments. Passengers on the bus included Loretta Lynn, Minnie Pearl, Patsy Kline, Flat & Scruggs, Grandpa Jones, Jr. Samples, Archie Campbell, Roy Clark, and Buck Owens. Some of the passengers disembarked the bus to visit while placing their orders, while several remained on board. Two car-hops went on the bus to take their orders. Marvin always joined those that did not get off the bus in order to greet them. On one occasion Minnie Pearl said, "Mr. Russell, would it be alright if I call you 'Marvin'?" "Of course!" he agreed.

Marvin spent three years traveling from Huntsville to

Van Nuys, California, White Sands, New Mexico, Aberdeen
Proving Grounds in Maryland, Homestead, Florida to Georgia to
New Jersey, and all over the country.

While traveling from El Paso, Texas to White Sands,
New Mexico, Marvin felt a pain in his chest which became
worse as the day went on. Marvin's friend drove him to El Paso,
Texas. He recovered in the hospital for six weeks when two G.I.
s from Fort Bliss arrived. They said, "Mr. Russell we have
something here for you to sign." Marvin inquired, "Do you
know where it came from?" They said, "Yes, it came from
Redstone arsenal." Marvin asked, "Did Rufas Porter send it?" to
which they replied in the affirmative. Marvin directed them to
put his name back on it and return it. Evidently, he wanted
Marvin to retire with a medical discharge. Marvin refused and
they left. Two months went by before he returned to Redstone
Arsenal. The colonel informed Marvin that he was grounded
and could not fly. Unexpectedly one day, the travel secretary
came in and said he was going to California. He said, "No, I
cannot. I am grounded." The colonel called him in and said he
had to have Marvin at the site in California and Marvin again
said, "I am grounded." The colonel called again and this time
said he ordered a car to pick him and Marvin up to see the
general. The general repeated the need for Marvin to travel to

California. Marvin sarcastically offered to go by train since he was grounded. The general said Marvin would be "ungrounded" and later that day headed out to Van Nuys to continue the work on the TSQ-73.

After all that he endured, Marvin had another close encounter many years after. Marvin felt something was not right with his heart while in the prison camp but did not get diagnosed with anything until many years later. Upon his return, doctors prescribed Quinidine for about ten years, and later switched to Endurol. But after switching doctors, they prescribed him Lopressor. At this time, Marvin operated two greenhouses and experienced trouble walking from them to the warehouse across the driveway. He told the doctor, "You're killing me!" The doctor replied that it was the lesser of two evils so he had to stay on the medicine.

One day later, in August of 1981, Marvin walked in the garden when all of a sudden he fell over and lost consciousness. Eventually, he came to and crawled to the barn in order to call his son Steve. When he finally arrived at the barn, Marvin was exhausted and disoriented and could hardly see the numbers on the telephone. He then crawled to the warehouse another forty feet away. Luckily, at that moment, his son happened to walk in and asked, "What's the matter, Dad?" At this point Marvin could not speak. Steve called the doctor and was told to get him to the Veteran's Hospital in Atlanta as soon as possible. Marvin traveled to the hospital with his wife Lois and his son Steve. Marvin was taken directly to the emergency room where he was given I.V.s in each arm and they searched for his chart. Marvin commented that if he could have talked he would have told them where his chart was located!

Marvin was not in complete control of his faculties and had limited ability to respond to questions. The nurse said that if he wanted something, Marvin should squeeze his hand, which he could not do. Next, they said to blink his eyes, of which he was capable. After asking Marvin which medications he was taking, the doctors realized he was taking the wrong ones. They declared, "Oh my God, get those I.V.s out!" Marvin then was taken to coronary care where he remembered hearing his own heart beat. When the doctors next took his blood pressure it read twenty-nine over twenty-two to which the doctor replied, "That is not pressure!" The doctor told Marvin that a temporary pacemaker must be inserted. Marvin said, "Doc, I need to talk about this." The doctor replied, "Talk, hell you're about to go!" The problem that arose next was that none of the doctors in the group had ever participated in pacemaker surgery. One intern assisted, inserting a pacemaker in a patient in New York City but no doctor had completed the surgery in its entirety. After multiple attempts to get the pacemaker inserted correctly, the head doctor asked, "Is it in yet?" The intern that helped with the surgery in New York replied, "Not quite. I either hit or missed the jugular and I'll have to come out and go in again." After some time had passed, the head doctor asked again, "Are you there yet?" The intern repeated, "Not quite." The other doctor said, "Turn it on anyway, we've already lost him." No beeps could be heard from the heart monitor. A few minutes later a beep was heard, and everyone in the room became excited, until the head doctor said, "That's not a heartbeat, it is a heart muscle reaction. There will be one or two more when he goes." Thirty seconds later there was a second beep. No one said anything. After the third beep, the doctor commented, "Maybe we've got him." The next memory Marvin has is when he woke up, whereupon the nurses fed him sugar and potassium.

While unconscious, Marvin believes he witnessed the entire procedure. Many people, during near death experiences claim they "saw the light," or felt the grace of God but ultimately survived. Marvin called it his 'out of body experience,' where it seemed like he watched what was happening from possibly a journey to heaven that was cut short. Marvin came close to death yet again, but apparently that was not God's plan!

Marvin Russell endured more than what multiple men put together experience in a lifetime. His family suffered not only through the Great Depression but also the Dust Bowl. They decided to stay on the farm and wait it out rather than take off for "greener pastures" in California and other places. When told his parents could not afford to pay for college, Marvin worked two jobs to ensure he walked away with an education. All he asked of his parents was a ride to the college.

He served proudly in the United States Army Air Corps and sacrificed thirteen months of his life in a prisoner of war camp. Marvin returned home, ready to start a life with his wife Lois on their farm when he almost lost his own life in a tragic explosion. Recovering from the burns that doctors said would be fatal, Marvin again attempted to resume life as normal. Tragedy struck again with the loss of his son days after a seemingly harmless mistake.

Thirty years of continued service to the United States Government provided travel and opportunities helping to ensure national security during the Cold War. During this time, Marvin also experienced a heart attack from which he recovered. Upon retiring, Marvin worked in greenhouses and operated a hardware store where he experienced more coronary trouble which almost resulted in death. Again he recovered. After all this, Marvin

Russell's life settled down somewhat, but he continued to face other ailments.

Marvin endured two broken hips and a broken back. Once he recovered from the second hip surgery, Marvin's doctors told him he could no longer stay in his house with stairs. As a result, he moved to "The Cottages" of Southern Plantation, in Loganville, Georgia, a retirement community where Marvin continues to embrace each day with his infectious laugh with countless friends and family by his side.

It is safe to say that no opportunity was ever just handed to Marvin Russell. Success that came his way resulted only from

Marvin, the social butterfly with both his home telephone and cell phone ringing at the same time!

life experiences and a determination to work hard. He never expected a handout from anyone and still does not to this day.

Now in his nineties, Marvin spends his time talking with friends, bugging the operator of the community where he lives, and speaking of his experiences. He has a hysterical sense of humor and a laugh that is simply contagious. We should all have his outlook on life.

His final comment in the interview reads:

"Going to heaven is like being in prison camp: you are not really sure what it's like unless you've been there and everyone will have a slightly different story. And I don't think we'll ever meet anyone that's been to heaven."

Epilogue

During the summer of 1995, I worked for the Penfield New York Parks and Recreation Department during their Fourth of July celebration. My job that day entailed ferrying older gentlemen to where they needed to be for the ceremony. I had just turned twenty-one the day before and was still feeling the effect of our own celebration the last evening. As I picked up these men and transported them from their parking spot to the main event area, I hate to say it, but I did not think for one second the reason why these men were there that day. I did not realize that they were World War II veterans participating in a ceremony marking their contributions to this nation's freedom. I thought more about the upcoming evening's festivities rather these former soldiers and what they participated in fifty some years earlier. I want to kick myself now. At that time, approximately five hundred World War II veterans died daily. I had the perfect opportunity to learn from the men that witnessed history but was apathetic. Many years later, in the early 2000s, I learned that over 1000 World War II vets died every day. I made it my cause to learn from as many as I possibly could. I think I have fulfilled that goal. If only I would have came to that same realization years before. The potential stories and history I could have heard...

Citations

1. History Book Committee. *Canton, Kansas: History of the Canton Community, 1864-1988.* Shawnee Mission, KS: Kes-Print, 1988.

2. "Company History." *Company History.* N.p., n.d. Web. 11 Feb. 2012. <http://www.emerson.com/en-us/about/overview/history/Pages/default.aspx>.

3. Colwell, James L. "MIDLAND ARMY AIR FIELD." *Texas State Historical Association (TSHA).* Texas State Historical Association, n.d. Web. 11 Feb. 2012. <http://www.tshaonline.org/handbook/online/articles/qbm02>.

4. "Military." *Kelly AFB.* N.p., 05 May 2011. Web. 18 Feb. 2012. <http://www.globalsecurity.org/military/facility/kelly.htm>.

5. "Kelly Field Historic District Aviation: From Sand Dunes to Sonic Booms." *National Park Service.* N.p., n.d. Web. 25 Feb. 2012. <http://www.nps.gov/nr/travel/aviation/kel.htm>.

6. "World War II - Airplane Mechanic School in Lincoln." *World War II - Airplane Mechanic School in Lincoln.* Nebraska State Historical Society, 20 Jan. 2006. Web. 11 Feb. 2012. <http://www.nebraskahistory.org/publish/publicat/timeline/wwii_airplane_mechanic_sch.htm>.

7. Kirshner, Jim. "Timeline Library." *HistoryLink.Org.* N.p., 31 Jan. 2010. Web. 25 Feb. 2012.

8. "Avon Park Air Force Station." *Military*. Global Security.Org, n.d. Web. 11 Feb. 2012. <http://www.globalsecurity. org/military/facility/apafr.htm>.

9. http://ww2pictures.akitajitsu.com/407th-bomb-squadron.html

10. http://ww2pictures.akitajitsu.com/planes-flying-on-bombing-run.html

11. Miller, Donald L. "The Bloody Hundredth." *Masters of the Air: America's Bomber Boys Who Fought the Air War against Nazi Germany*. New York: Simon & Schuster, 2006. 6. Print.

12. Anesi, Chuck. "United States Strategic Bombing Survey: Summary Report (European War)." *United States Strategic Bombing Survey: Summary Report (European War)*. N.p., 1997. Web. 25 Feb. 2012. <http://www.anesi. com/ussbs02.htm>.

13. "Henschel & Son Manufacturer." *Wehrmacht History 1935-1945*. N.p., n.d. Web. 11 Feb. 2012. <http://www. wehrmacht-history.com/manufacturers/henschel-manufacturer.htm>.

14. Klaube, Frank R. "Kassel-An Outline of the City's Development." *Kassel.de*. Kassel Marketing GmbH, n.d. Web. 25 Feb. 2012. <http://www.kassel. de/englisch/history/>.

15. Bauer, Dan F. "The Hamm Massacre." *91st Bomb Group*. N. p., n.d. Web. 25 Feb. 2012. <http://www.91stbombgroup. com/91st_tales/18_hamm_massacre.pdf>.

16. http://www.wwiiaircraftperformance.org/24april44.html

17. "Arizona Wing of the Commemorative Air Force." *Arizona Wing of the CAF*. N.p., n.d. Web. 25 Feb. 2012. <http://www.azcaf.org/pages/crew.html>.

18. http://www.azcaf.org/pages/crew.html

19. "German POW Camps with 303rd BG(H) Prisoners." *Hell's Angels 303rd Bomb Group (H)*. N.p., n.d. Web. 25 Feb. 2012. <http://www.303rdbg.com/pow-camps.html>.

20. "Convention Relative to the Treatment of Prisoners of War. Geneva, 27 July 1929." *International Humanitarian Law -Geneva Convention Prisoners of War 1929*. International Committee of the Red Cross, 2005. Web. 25 Feb. 2012. <http://www.icrc.org/ihl.nsf/full/305?opendocument>.

21. http://www.b24.net/pow/stalag17.htm#photos

22. http://www.b24.net/pow/stalag17.htm#photos

23. http://www.stalag17b.com/rules.htm#photos

24. http://www.bobpenoyer.com/pow-stalag17b-map.jpg (http://www.bobpenoyer.com/pow-stalag17b-map.jpg)

25. "History." *Stalag 17 B*. N.p., n.d. Web. 11 Feb. 2012. <http://www.stalag17b.com/history.html>.

26. "Convention Relative to the Treatment of Prisoners of War. Geneva, 27 July 1929." *International Humanitarian Law -Geneva Convention Prisoners of War 1929.* International Committee of the Red Cross, 2005. Web. 25 Feb. 2012. <http://www.icrc.org/ihl.nsf/full/305? opendocument>.

27. Ethier, Eric. "Stalag 17-B." *America in WWII.* 310 Publishing, LLC., n.d. Web. 25 Feb. 2012. <http://www. americainwwii.com/articles/stalag-17-b/>.

28. http://www.b24.net/pow/stalag17.htm%23photos

29. http://www.b24.net/pow/stalag17.htm%23photos

30. Ethier, Eric. "Stalag 17-B." *America in WWII.* 310 Publishing, LLC., n.d. Web. 11 Feb. 2012. <http://www. americainwwii.com/articles/stalag-17-b/>.

31. Ethier, Eric. "Stalag 17-B." *America in WWII.* 310 Publishing, LLC., n.d. Web. 11 Feb. 2012. <http://www. americainwwii.com/articles/stalag-17-b/>.

32. Ethier, Eric. "Stalag 17-B." *America in WWII.* 310 Publishing, LLC., n.d. Web. 11 Feb. 2012. <http://www. americainwwii.com/articles/stalag-17-b/>.

33. http://www.b24.net/pow/stalag17.htm%23photos

34. http://lcweb2.loc.gov/diglib/vhp/story/loc.natlib.afc2001001. 01202/enlarge?ID=pm0024001&page=1

35. Ethier, Eric. "Stalag 17-B." *America in WWII*. 310
    Publishing, LLC., n.d. Web. 11 Feb. 2012. <http://www.
    americainwwii.com/articles/stalag-17-b/>.

36. Ethier, Eric. "Stalag 17-B." *America in WWII*. 310
    Publishing, LLC., n.d. Web. 25 Feb. 2012. <http://www.
    americainwwii.com/articles/stalag-17-b/>.

37. http://stalag17b.ning.com/photo/pow-red-cross-parcels?
    context=latest

38. http://www.303rdbg.com/pow-camps.html (http://www.
    303rdbg.com/pow-camps.html

39. Hatton, Greg. "AMERICAN PRISONERS OF WAR IN
    GERMANY STALAG 17b." *WWW.B24.NET*.
    MILITARY INTELLIGENCE SERVICE WAR
    DEPARTMENT, n.d. Web. 25 Feb. 2012. <http://www.
    b24.net/pow/stalag17.htm>.

40. Hatton, Greg. "AMERICAN PRISONERS OF WAR IN
    GERMANY STALAG 17b." *WWW.B24.NET*.
    MILITARY INTELLIGENCE SERVICE WAR
    DEPARTMENT, n.d. Web. 25 Feb. 2012. <http://www.
    b24.net/pow/stalag17.htm>.

41. Courtesy of the Canton Pilot

Front cover: http://www.bobpenoyer.com/pow-stalag17b-map.
    jpg

Back cover: http://www.303rdbga.com/pow-camps-map.jpg